Rage that Spans Generations

Aponia's Journey to Restoration

Belinda M. Alexander-Ashley

ISBN: 978-1-961392-51-9

Note: The book *Rage that Spans Generations* is a work of historical fiction and does not attempt to replicate characters known or unknown to the author.

Dedication

This book is dedicated to those visionaries, educators, historians, and administrators committed to creating a brighter future for the next generation.

Acknowledgement

Thank you to my wonderful husband, Joey, and my children,
Olajuwon and Joy, for their unconditional support and insight.
Special thanks to my parents, Thomas and Gladys Alexander, Sr., for
always providing shoulders to stand on. To my ceaseless cheerleaders
who never leave my thoughts and prayers include Bruce Alexander
Sr., Larry Abernathy, Leland and Demytrea Ashley, Clarence "Rent"
Jackson, Wilma and Mose McNeese, Anna Cunningham, Sharon and
William "Bill" Hodges as well as the countless others who I was not
able to include. Thank you.

About the Author

Belinda Alexander-Ashley, Ph.D., is an independent researcher committed to the mantra, "It's never too late to forge a new future". After working more than twenty-two years in the federal probation system, she learned the importance of second chances and adaptation. She pivoted after retiring to reimagine a new journey as a writer highlighting the traumas experienced by past and future generations learning to equip themselves to overcome by engaging in therapy, meditation, connecting to nature, and focusing on objects that help them to see beyond barriers. While not all cultures advocate for professional assistance or therapy, the author hopes to normalize the use of processes that equip the next generation for what is to come. Additionally, it is hoped that others will join in this endeavor to strengthen the legacy left for others.

Table of Contents

Chapter One

She could feel the flame begin to intensify, singeing the edges of her mind. Her brain felt like it was immersed in a churning stew inside her skull. It was beginning to happen more frequently and she was having trouble controlling the anger and rage when it started. Her mother had labeled the angry outbursts as "the unprovoked rage" because her reactions to little things were overblown and disproportionate.

However, Aponia's boyfriend, Jett Franklin, understood her perfectly. He accepted her with all her imperfections. Why couldn't her family understand? Why didn't they want her to be happy? Jett made her happy. He was her champion and her guiding light during the darkest days of her life!

No one around her understood what she felt for Jett. She didn't understand him on occasion, but the two had finally connected to one another at the same time. They had always been dating other people until recently. Aponia thought about his long lanky body, golden skin, wavy hair, and knee-melting smile. She couldn't help but smile at the thought. Sure, he was a flirt with other girls, but he liked her best. Aponia kept that in a special part of her mind. No one else was allowed to talk about him without experiencing her wrath. She couldn't take one more snide comment about Jett.

Then, it happened! Valerie Monarch with her curly dark hair pulled back in a tail at her nape said the awful words, "Jett is a flirt." Her mother put her hands in the back pockets of her blue jeans as her thin green sweater clung to her upper body softening her girlish appearance. "Facts were facts and you need to accept that if you intend to date him," her mother stated as a matter-of-fact. "You are living in a fantasy world, baby girl."

Valerie Monarch touched her daughter's cheek as Aponia pulled away from her touch as if she'd been burned.

Her touch hurt Aponia's heart if not her face. The room seemed colder, whiter, and heartless to Aponia. Tears threatened to leak from her eyes. Aponia could not accept the words. They were not true. If they were, where did that leave her? This could not possibly be real. She had to get away. Jett had professed his love for Aponia often enough whether anyone else believed him or not. Aponia believed enough for all of them.

The feelings within began to build first from a slow flickering flame to a raging fire that threatened to scorch her scalp with its heat. Her body radiated in place starting with her small converse sneakers, through her blue jeans, through her favorite pink Mulan t-shirt and up through her head and out through her scalp. As Aponia stood on tip toes to her full five-foot-four-inch height, her reddish freckles nearly jumped off her golden face as she yelled, "I hate you! You are ruining my life! You don't understand our love!" Her eyes bugged out and Aponia stomped back and forth trying to reign herself back in. It wasn't working today.

"Don't be so dramatic, Poni!" Valerie responded picking up discarded undergarments and clothing from her daughter's floor and bed calmly moving around Aponia's vibrating body. This was not new for her mother. She'd seen all this before, but was ill-equipped to deal with it. So, she did what she always did when her daughter was acting out, pretend the behavior wasn't happening. "Get a hold of yourself before you're grounded until your 30 years old! Do you hear me, Poni!"

Aponia stomped back and forth across the floor as the fury continued to build with each step. With eyes bugged out, fists pumping back and forth at her sides, she yelled, "Jett loves me and I love him! Get over it, mother!"

Although Aponia and her boyfriend, Jett Franklin, had been friends since they were in first grade, they had only recently began dating. When he was younger, Jett had been known for his flirtatious nature and loose morals where dating was concerned. However, all that changed when he and Aponia began dating. He committed himself to making Aponia happy. However, her family and friends' comments were beginning to make her question her own commitment to Jett. Did he change or did she simply accept the status quo? She didn't want to believe she had become blind to Jett's behavior. She chose to believe the best of him. That was what a good girlfriend did. Didn't she?

Valerie Monarch dropped her hands to her side and stopped to look more closely at her daughter, who seemed to have steam rolling from her ears and heat pumping off her body. Valerie had been divorced for several years after constant fighting with her husband, Ethan Monarch. Even though the husband and wife constantly fought during their marriage, both loved their three children dearly and vowed to co-parent as friends. Since the divorce, they had presented a united front to their kids.

In the past when the rage had emerged, there had been no one Aponia could confide her fears in. She remembered once responding to her teacher Ms. Williams' request for her to take her seat in the middle of their history class of twenty students. Then it started; the blinding anger clouded her mind to the point that it took over her voice, stating, "You are not my mother! You can't tell me what to do!"

If that was not bad enough, Aponia put her hands on her hips and smiled at her classmates daring her favorite teacher to say different.

Aponia watched as Ms. Williams straightened to her full five-foot-ten-inch height, looked down her spectacles that sat on the tip of her nose just to the point of falling, and focused her brown eyed gaze at Aponia. In those eyes, Aponia saw disappointment like she'd never seen in the past from the kind teacher.

"You are correct that I am not your mother and it is your choice to obey my requests," Ms. Williams said just above a whisper. Moving from behind her desk and leaning on the front of the wooden rectangular desk scarred with years of classroom experiences, she silently waited. Her long trouser clad legs were crossed at the ankle and her arms were folded across her chest. This was a standoff. Even though Aponia knew that she was in the wrong, she was embarrassed and ashamed to turn tail and run. How could she back down without appearing weak to her friends? The ball was in her court.

Everyone in class stared at her. Ms. Williams continued to wait as Aponia's rage dissipated and embarrassment increased. No one spoke for what seemed like an eternity. Very slowly Aponia shrunk back from her words and took her seat quietly. Class resumed as if Aponia had not made a fool of herself in front of her classmates. After class was another story.

There were other times that her rage had gotten her sent to the Dean's Office where her parents were called. The disappointment Aponia saw in her mother and father's eyes made her feel ashamed and embarrassed. They had taught her better and she was making a mockery of their efforts. Her life was out of control.

Fourteen-year-old Aponia Monarch with golden skin, curly dark brown hair and cinnamon freckles that reflected her Irish heritage was a force of nature. Her mother and father taught their children to be proud of their mixed heritage and strong genealogical roots. Because of the small birthmark on her left shoulder that resembled a butterfly, her parents named her Aponia, meaning butterfly, in the hope that their beautiful child's life would be transformational like one.

Her older brother, Solomon, younger sister, Sophia, and their mother lived in a white and red brick single story ranch-style home on Jefferson Street. Most of the homes on Jefferson Street were single family homes that were inhabited by blue collar families struggling to make ends meet. It was considered safe within the small Honey Springs community.

Honey Springs is a small town in northeast Oklahoma. The population boasts a whopping 2,516 residents, most of whom have lived in and around the area for more than 100 years. As older residents pass away, younger people move out of area for more lucrative career endeavors and retirees return to their family home. Honey Springs is approximately five square miles northeast of Checotah, Oklahoma. Although many great residents have graced its borders, Honey Springs' greatest claim to fame is the Battle of Honey Springs, which occurred on July 17, 1863. History books did little to create a legacy for the next generations. There was a paucity of historical accounts of the soldiers who fought and died in the battle especially the former slaves and Native Americans.

The Monarch family did more than most families to create and honor their legacy during Memorial Day celebrations. Serving to educate and honor those that came before, the annual celebration included cleaning debris and grass from grave sites, sharing family stories, and indulging in large community picnics. Aponia thought the family talked too much about that history. "What did old battles and sad memories of death and destruction have to do with building a new future?" she often asked herself.

From as far back as any Monarch family member could remember, the family had been held as slaves in Arkansas. They traveled on foot as escaped slaves from Arkansas to Honey Springs, Oklahoma, which was a part of Indian Territory at that time. On November 16, 1907, Indian Territory became the state of Oklahoma. For generations, the Monarch family-owned property in and around the area first as farmers and then moving into town to improve access to education and resources for their children.

Aponia's parents met in elementary school and had been childhood sweet hearts. They eventually married and had three children. With time, the family experienced life's difficulties. They divorced three years prior, improving the atmosphere in the house and restoring a calm and peace for the family.

Valerie Monarch blamed herself for her daughter's anger and Aponia occasionally used the guilt to get what she wanted. "Gotta use some things to your advantage," Aponia mumbled more to herself than anyone else pushing her round glasses up further onto her nose. She didn't know where the anger came from, but she was aware that it was getting worse and more uncontrollable. In her mind, once she and Jett were happily married, the rage would dissipate and float away. That was the way it should work, right?

Her mother's guilt centered around her husband's infidelity. Although not her fault, Valerie felt she should have been paying more attention to her husband resulting in the situation. It was faulty thinking at best on her part. Ethan Monarch had been remorseful that his actions caused the marriage's demise and reconciled to be a perfect father. Subsequently, he and his wife agreed that their constant fighting had been a contributing factor to their daughter's anger and rage. The infidelity would never be shared with their children. Both accepted their responsibility in the divorce. Since that time, they had become better co-parents and friends. Their children only saw the united front presented by their parents.

Valerie Monarch suspected her daughter's outrageous behavior may be the result of her seeking male attention to validate her self-worth. Jett Franklin had been the one to provide that attention. As a younger child, Jett never paid any attention to her daughter until the last several months. Then all of a sudden, the two were inseparable and in love. Valerie chided herself for being so vocal about Jett to her daughter. However, she had wanted to warn her daughter about what she perceived were his ill intentions. Although well intended, Valerie Monarch's words seemed to have the opposite effect driving her daughter to increase her loyalty to Jett.

Valerie and Ethan Monarch had gone to high school with Tesha Franklin, Jett's mother. Tesha had gotten pregnant in high school at the age of fifteen-years-old by John Rossi, who was nineteen-years-old. Tesha suffered the stigma of being an unwed teenage mother while John Rossi walked away from his responsibility claiming that he never touched Tesha. Jett's mother was a beauty in her own right, but her parents allowed her freedom to date as she wished and make adult decisions where her teenage life was concerned. Not wanting to be judgmental, Valerie was careful to refrain from negative comments about Tesha or her parenting style.

John Rossi, who was known to take advantage of teenage girls with their tender feelings, pretended that he'd never known Tesha beyond casual friends. After her son was born, Tesha dropped out of school and worked in Jona's Family Diner, located within walking distance from their home. John Rossi added Jett to his tally of children, three boys and one girl.

Now, Tesha Franklin lives with her son on Confederate Way in a small mobile home badly in need of repairs. Like his mother, Jett was allowed freedom to date, have sleepovers, and attend school at his own discretion. As Aponia can attest, Jett frequently chose to stay at home from school citing frequent headaches and back pain. Valerie feared for her daughter's well-being citing Jett's influence. She was suspicious of Jett's recent interest in her daughter.

When her head cleared, Aponia stormed into her bedroom, which she shared with her younger sister, Sophia. The small room was painted a soft green with twin beds on opposite sides of the room, a small closet in the southeast corner, a small chest of drawers next to the door and a toy box filled the space along the back wall. Aponia threw herself into the rail back rocking chair passed down to her by her grandmother which sat in front of the window. Her thin body flopped into the chair with her arms folded across her chest. Her legs crossed at the knee with one leg swinging frantically back and forth as her oversized feet rocked in a quick rhythm of its own. She rolled her eyes skyward. Her mother glared at her daughter in warning.

"Done?" Valerie asked angrily. "You have made your point! Now, mind your manners Aponia Arminda Monarch!" Aponia recognized when she had reached her mother's limit with her bad behavior. Her mother's use of her full name was a definite sign.

Valerie Monarch had perfected the death glare with her children. Aponia dropped her arms to her sides and looked anywhere, but at her mother's face. Her expression clearly said end of discussion. The conversation may have ended for her mother, but Aponia definitely had more to say. "Get yourself together, Poni!" her mother stated closing the door behind her with a loud click.

Solomon Franklin, who had been listening from his room next door, made his ghostly appearance in the hallway outside Aponia's door after determining the hall was clear. He cupped his ear with his hand and leaned his long lanky body into the door listening for sounds inside. He could hear the creaking of the rocking chair and imagined his sister was blowing off steam. Solomon didn't bother to knock because he was sure no response would come. Opening the door quietly, he cracked the door just enough to see inside. Before he could focus on his sister, a thwack sounded on the back of the door. Solomon felt the heavy decorative pillow hit the back of the door and slide down to the floor. He slammed the door closed avoiding any other items thrown by his sister.

When he turned around, he was greeted with the curious presence of his little sister also known as the "Brat". She was licking a blue lollypop that left her tongue an unearthly blue color. She tilted her head sideways and asked, "What ya' doing?" The pint-sized princess was the spitting image of her mother with dark braids that hung past her shoulders, green eyes that begged for attention and a dainty little denim blue overall short set trimmed in soft pink ruffles. She was a cute little pixie that was hard to stay mad at.

Solomon grinned big, "Waiting for you. Poni was just asking for you."

Unsuspecting, Sophia opened the door with a big grin on her face showing her blue tongue and dimpled cheeks. Thwack! A pillow hit her in the middle of her forehead. Sophia expression was slow to change as it went from smiling to screaming, "MOOOMMMM! Poni hit me!" She tore down the hall at a run like her little overalls were on fire in search of her mother. And it didn't take her long to find her. Solomon could hear the Brat sharing her exchange with her sister.

Solomon smiled to himself, "My work here is done." He quietly turned and went back into his room to avoid the fray that he was sure would come. Like clockwork, he heard the quick clicks of his mother's sandals slapping the wooden floor returning back down the hall with Sophia in tow. Solomon couldn't see what was going on, but could imagine what was happening as he listened to the raised voices. For him, this was family.

Solomon was a brainy kid popular among the boys in tenth grade. He was captain of the chest club and editor of the Honey Spring High School Newsletter. Unlike most brainy kids, Solomon was athletic and good with relationships that put other students at ease. However, he had his moments at home when he just wanted a little chaos to spice up his day. His sisters were the perfect candidates to become recipients of his good-natured fun.

Lately, he was becoming increasingly concerned with Aporia's outbursts at home and in school. Solomon also didn't like the fact that Jett was paying so much attention to Aponia and his classmate, Jenny Carpenter. Neither were a bad sort. However, he didn't like the idea that Jett may be dating Jenny and his sister at the same time.

"Poni!" her mother yelled. "You know better! Don't you dare take your frustrations out on your little sister." Valerie Monarch's small body radiated heat as she was encapsulated in the negative energy swirling about her eldest daughter.

Sophia on the other hand innocently sucked on her lollypop as tears leaked from her eyes. Aponia was always amazed at how her little sister could summon tears without notice and dry them as quickly. When her mother turned to leave, Sophia licked her tongue at her sister for good measure. Her little body wiggled as her body and head went opposite directions to exaggerate the tongue licking.

"Sophia Joylin Monarch, I can see you!" her mother clamped a hand on her arm and pulled her down the hall behind her. "You are not to go down there and tease your sister." Aponia could hear her mother's voice as she dragged her little sister away. She was amazed that not much got past her mother. It made her wonder if she had eyes in the back of her head.

Once she was alone, the room became quiet again. The lights above softened to reflect the sunshine streaming in from the windows. The anger that had churned like a stew in her head now slowly left her body like a syrup being poured from a bottle allowing its contents to seep out slowly. The air in the room cooled from the heat that had been pumping from her body into the room. As her head cleared, she noted that the half made twin bed on one wall looked chaotic compared to Sophia's neatly made one on the opposite wall. The chest of drawers next to the rocking chair between the beds seemed enormous from the chair. The room smelled like cinnamon that mom used in the oatmeal cookies. Things were back to normal again. Or as normal as she could remember.

Aponia didn't like the yelling and shouting, but didn't know how to stop it. Most of the yelling and screaming lately had been related to her actions and behaviors. None of this was on purpose, but her control was slowly stretching to a misshapen form that she no longer recognized. How did she make the chaos and anger stop? The world kept spinning out of control and she didn't know how to make it stop.

She'd heard her mother and father disrespecting each other with foul language during their marriage or so she thought. Some of the fights were about her. Aponia felt guilty that her behavior had impacted her parents' marriage. Solomon had once blamed her for her parent's divorce. It was hurtful. Apologizing, the disagreement ended without hard feelings.

Desperate situations that she had caused required desperate responses. She had to make a decision that would change the trajectory of her life. If she ran away, she could marry Jett and they would live happily ever after. There would be no need to yell and scream because they'd love each other and raise children in a loving environment. That was the plan.

Chapter Two

Aponia carefully dressed in the dark wearing baggy blue jeans, an orange t-shirt with flowers in the middle, a worn blue jean jacket and red converse. Her brown face sprinkled with slightly darker freckles reflected the light that sifted in between the slats of the mini blinds covering the window. She looked down at herself carefully inventorying things that she would need as she prepared to run away from home. No one understood how hard she tried to fit in with her siblings. The easy-going Solomon with his darker complexion, green eyes, and protective nature made Aponia smile to herself. She would miss his long slim form and joking nature designed to help her to forget her problems. She had to admit that he was a good big brother.

However, she would not miss the perfect baby girl, Sophia aka the Brat. She put her finger into her mouth mimicking a gagging motion. Everyone regarded Sophia as a beauty. Dark wavy hair, honey colored skin, green eyes similar to her mother, and no freckles that drove Aponia mad. If Sophia smiled, the whole world and everyone in it smiled with her. The skies opened up and sang hallelujah! To her fourteen-year-old mind, that was what Sophia's world felt like. If she was unhappy, everyone moved heaven and earth to make Sophia smile. "Uggg!" Aponia thought to herself quietly gagging on the thought. She wondered if everyone felt the same about their perfect little sisters. Time to move, she thought as she neared the window.

"No regrets," she mumbled to herself. "No looking back." Aponia gave the small dark room with its two twin beds and matching Mulan bed spreads one last look. She could smell the faint smell of apples and cinnamon that her mother used on their apple crisp snacks. It was the smells of home. Her favorite Disney character, Mulan, would not hesitate to go to war for what she believed. If Mulan could do that, Aponia felt she could too. Well maybe not to war, but she could stand up for what she believed and the one she loved.

She believed in Jett, even if the two had not been dating for very long. They had been childhood friends. Of course, Jett wasn't very nice to her when they were young, constantly pulling her hair and calling her four eyes. "Is that the way boys showed girls that they liked them," she thought back to herself. If that were the case, he definitely loved Aponia and several other little girls.

Two months ago, Jett looked at her and said he saw the beautiful young woman that she had become. She hadn't noticed that she had transformed into a swan until Jett mentioned it. Although flirtatious with other girls, he always claimed that she had been the most beautiful.

"That was what was most important," Aponia thought to herself. She and Jett had talked about running away several months ago. At that time, it had not been a consideration for Aponia. Jett didn't seem overly serious about it either if she was being honest with herself. What would he think about running away without discussing a plan before they left? The time was right and Aponia could no longer endure the anger and rage that churned inside her. Jett had to understand the urgency, didn't he? She convinced herself that all would be well with her decision made.

Aponia tried to convince herself that Jett would be agreeable to her decision to runaway together. They had talked about getting married in the future, buying a house and having children that they would love beyond reason. Wasn't he the one who had encouraged her to run away with him if she ever became fed up with her family's nonsense? He promised to love and protect her from everyone. Today was that day. She and Jett would run away together and live happily ever after. He said he had a plan and would work hard supporting her. One last look around, she closed her eyes, said a little prayer and slid the window up quietly. The alarm dinged softly indicating that a window had been raised.

As alarm dinged, an automated voice indicated that a window had been opened. "Aponia, did you open the window?" her mother's voice permeated the darkness. She had forgotten about the alarm as she stood statue still. Sophia lay asleep across the room.

She called back with more calm that she really felt, "Yes, the room was stuffy and hot. I wanted to let in some fresh air." Aponia answered watching Sophia turn repositioning herself in sleep.

"I will come in before I go to bed and let it back down so that you and Sophie remain safe," her mother added. Aponia smiled at her sometimes over protective mother.

"Ok," she responded as she pushed the screen away from the frame. Dropping her dark green backpack out the window with a thud, Aponia slid out and down to the ground landing on the lush green grass. In the dark, the grass almost looked black in the night although she recognized the feel of the thick grass that muffled her steps. She waited for her eyes to adjust to the darkness before moving from the shadows. Looking around to see if anyone noticed her, she squatted low and quickly replaced the screen in the frame dashing into the night. The night air was cool and crisp.

Jett lived one block north and two blocks east on Confederate Way. His block was part of a mobile home community where residents frequently moved for better career opportunities. Aponia noticed the inky blackness around her in the absence of street lamps and the call of distant locusts. The sounds of nature were overwhelming causing her to pull her jacket closer to her body. It was not the cold that made her shake, it was fear of what may be lurking in the darkness. She hid herself behind a huge oak tree with a hanging swing in her front yard. Looking around for movement, she gathered her courage and ran down the street with her backpack on her back. The straps of the bag rode high throwing off her balance causing her to run with a slight rowing motion. The air was crisp and clean following the rain from the previous day. A hooting owl caused her to run faster.

Her legs tired as she passed Ariyana's house one block east on Union Boulevard. Ariyana was Aponia's best friend and confidante. She would miss her friend's dark round face, flowing braids of brown, black and blond. She hadn't the confidence to tell her friend of her plans to run away. Ariyana would surely stop Aponia and discourage her from placing her trust in Jett. Ariyana complained that Jett was self-centered, flirtatious and cared for no one except himself. She disagreed and found him to be a gentleman that always had her best interest. Why were so many people distrustful of Jett. Sure, he had made mistakes, but who hadn't? Aponia willed herself to stay focused.

Aponia finally saw the outline of Jett's home come into view. It was a small dimly lit mobile home on the corner of Old Depot Road and Confederate Way. The outline of the home reminded her of a railroad box car with two dimly lit windows across the front. Stiff brown grass dotted the front yard along the paved driveway that was pitted with ruts and holes making running impossible. The front porch was a small wooden structure that looked like it was made more for a small boat dock. When they were younger, they often pretended they were on a ship watching for whales and sharks in the ocean. A tan strip on the brown siding lined the bottom of the home and provided a guide for Aponia to follow to the back side of the trailer where she knew she would find Jett's bedroom.

Once on the backside of the home, she stopped and listened for voices in the dark. Nothing. Rubbing the glass with her sleeve, she peaked in the small, dirt coated window. No movement save for a black straggly cat named Scrappy. Jett had found the cat in an abandoned building fending off two larger dogs who were trying to relieve him of the remains of a rat that he'd found. Afterward, Jett took him home to live with his family. Now, he lounged on a pile of clothes inside a basket next to a door lit by a hallway light.

With her head on swivel, she observed clothes and food containers lining the floor of Jett's bedroom. The bed was pushed against the wall next to the window, so she was unsure if Jett was lying in the bed. Tap, tap, tap. She knocked softly on the window frame. No answer. Tap, tap, tap. No answer. She sat down next to the window in the dark trying to formulate a plan in her head. She never considered that he might not be at home. Settling into the dark, she fumbled in her pocket for her cell phone. She typed in his number and waited for him to answer. Jett answered on the third ring explaining that he was out with a friend. He agreed to meet Aponia outside his window in 10 minutes.

As she sat in the dark hiding from prying eyes, she saw a mangy little puppy watching her surreptitiously. The puppy's fur was so matted that he looked like he had short dread locks. Aponia reached for the dirt covered pup. Bearing small sharp teeth, he scooted back in the dark. Remembering pieces of dried turkey in her bag, she took off her back pack and retrieved the turkey. The pup looked at her curiously. Eyeing the meat like it was the first he'd seen in a very longtime, the pup pawed it trying to shake it loose from her hand. He sniffed it and pushed back. Aponia tossed the turkey into the dark next to him. The hungry little pup gobbled it up without chewing. He watched for more to come his way.

Aponia heard Jett before she could see his long dark form moving in the night. His broad shoulders and narrow hips were familiar as he moved in his easy gait. "Poni?" he whispered. Aponia responded by touching his arm lightly. In response, he groped for her hand and pulled her from the darkness next to the skirting of the trailer. The little pup followed hoping for more food.

"Who is your friend?" Jett asked kissing her lightly on her cheek.

"I found him underneath the trailer hiding. I think he is hungry." She smiled scooping the pup into her arms.

"You and your friend come along," Jett smiled pulling her around to the front of the trailer toward the wooden stairs leading to the front door. Two steps led up to the small flat landing surrounded by peeling wood rails. Although Aponia had noticed the peeling paint in the past, today it pricked her attention and made her wonder why no one had taken the time to paint it.

Beyond the small foyer of six discolored marble tiles, the living room was littered with newspapers strewn across the coffee table and unfolded clothes on the sofa. His mother, Ms. Tesha, was nowhere in sight. Generally, she worked the evening shift at the diner. The kitchen was quiet with dishes stacked neatly in the sink and a lone yellow bulb glowing above the stove. The air smelled of stale marijuana smoke and air freshener, a sickly-sweet mixture.

Jett pulled her along the narrow hall toward his bedroom. Green shag carpet lined the hallway and pictures of Jett when he was younger lined the walls leading to his bedroom. His smile as a child was magical. She was sentimental at the thought. Smiling at the face looking back at her, Aponia found his pictures adorable. Once inside his bedroom, Jett released her arm and motioned for her to sit on the bed.

The pup growled at Scrappy who was upset at having her nap interrupted. Aponia moved discarded clothing from the bed unsure if they were clean or dirty and sat. Jett pulled a chair from his desk next to the door and sat in front of her. The pup squirmed hoping for more food. Jett took a discarded piece of chicken from a dish on his desk and watched the pup tear into it ravenously.

Both Jett and Aponia looked at each other expectantly. He clearly had no idea why Aponia would be at his home this late at night. She also found it odd that he had been out late while his mother was out. Valerie Monarch kept a taut ship requiring that her children be at home and accounted for at night especially.

"Where is your mom?" Aponia asked curiously. She didn't want to cause Jett trouble with his mother. Surely, having a girl in his bedroom especially at night unchaperoned would be hard to explain.

"Out!" Jett yelled at Scrappy who had trying to sneak around them to get a bit closer to the pup. The cat responded with an angry sniff and left the room. "What are you doing here?"

"You said if I ever wanted to run away that I should let you know," Aponia explained sheepishly. "Today is the day."

Jett smiled and rubbed his chin. "Never actually thought you would do it," he commented assessing his options. "I guess we are running away tonight. What is your plan?"

Aponia looked puzzled, "I thought you had a plan." Jett frowned and took out his cell phone. "Excuse me for a moment." He closed the door to the bedroom and Aponia leaned toward the door listening to his whispers from the kitchen just off the hallway. She heard Jett talking to someone about an unexpected complication and needing to help a friend out. The person on the phone was not happy because Jett apologized profusely and said he would get rid of the problem. Aponia didn't like the sound of that. She wasn't anyone's problem. Jett was quiet for a time and commented to someone named "Jay" that he would work something out.

A few minutes later, Jett reentered the room with his empty back pack. He began stuffing clothes from the bed and floor into the backpack. After placing toiletries and other items in the backpack, he motioned for her to follow. She wanted to ask about the person on the phone, but felt it best to let it go for now.

"Ready to go?" Jett said motioning Aponia to follow him. She couldn't gauge his mood, but he didn't seem excited to be running away with her. He turned off lights as they left each room. This seemed odd to her since he acted like this was just like any other day. Something was off about the situation and she was becoming more and more uncomfortable.

"Won't your mother worry if you are not at home when she returns?" Aponia asked as he completed his lock up process. The pup wiggled in Aponia's arms, but she held firm. The pup's small legs were not long enough to keep a fast pace, so she carried the feisty pup. Underneath his fur, she could feel the healing scars.

"Why?" Jett asked as he pushed on the closed front door to ensure that it was locked behind him. She followed him down the porch and onto the paved driveway. "My mom respects me and allows me to come and go as I please."

"You're only fifteen-years-old."

"Almost grown," Jett protested. "My mom had me when she was fifteen-years-old. She was on her own and we did fine."

Aponia was astonished. She'd never heard this story. She was fourteen and her mother didn't see her as nearly grown. Maybe Ms. Tesha had to grow up fast with a baby? Jett seemed happy with his circumstances, so maybe she could get used to the freedom as well?

"Where are we going?" Aponia asked when they followed Old Depot Road to Gentry Street. This was a part of town that she didn't often see before or after dark although it was just blocks away. People seemed to be always loitering on the corners selling specialty clothing, tennis shoes, jewelry or smoking cigarettes. Her mother and father told her to stay away from the area fearing she'd be exposed to criminal activity. As they walked, Aponia placed her hand in Jett's and walked closer to him. She cuddled the pup in her other hand holding him close to her body. The pup sensed something different because he stopped wiggling, put his nose in the air, and whimpered softly.

"No worries. I'll protect you." Jett smiled and enfolded Aponia in a warm embrace before continuing down the block to a dark three-story building. No lights were on the first floor and dim lights shown through thin curtains on the second and third floors. Jett pulled on the heavy metal door as it creaked loudly opening to a dimly lit foyer and hallway. A sickly yellow bulb glowed at the far end of the hall making the surroundings look like a creepy cave from a horror flick.

Aponia clenched her hand into a fist as she held to the back of Jett's t-shirt partially hiding herself behind him. It took a moment for her eyes to adjust to the lighting inside the foyer leading to a hallway with two scarred doors on either side. The pup burrowed closer to Aponia's body. The air smelled of unwashed bodies, cigarette and marijuana smoke mixed with rotting food. Aponia placed the lower part of her shirt across her face to protect her nose from the smells. Jett stopped momentarily and continued to the door on the right. The numbers 122 appeared outside the dark colored door scarred with gouges and what looked like shoe kick imprints.

Jett rapped twice on the door. In response, the door opened a crack and a brown red rimmed eye peered out. "What?" a gruff voice asked.

"It's me, Jett," he responded just above a whisper.

"What do you want?" a gravelly voice asked.

"I need a room," Jett stated as the door opened revealing the dark bulky form of a mixed-race man wearing a dirty wife beater t-shirt and black baggy shorts. Dark broken down house shoes with the backs smashed down covered the front portion of his feet. She looked around to the neatly kept apartment. A small blue sofa flanked by a blue and white striped love seat sat in front of the huge flat screen television. The man pulled a key from a hook on the wall just opposite the front door and handed it to Jett. The man looked more closely at Aponia paying close attention to her hips and upper body. Aponia stepped behind Jett in response to the scrutiny.

"Same terms as always," the man stated continuing to look at Aponia. Jett nodded agreement before turning to leave. Aponia looked over her shoulder and didn't like the way the man continued to watch her. The scrutiny made her feel creepy like she was being sized up for the main course at a buffet.

"Later, Dex," Jett waved closing the door behind him. The man smiled like a lion watching his prey.

Dexter Palmer known to his friends and associates as "Dex" had owned the three-story building for more than ten years. He had come to own the building when a couple of drug dealers had a violent confrontation and one killed the other. The survivor owned the building and was willing to sell the building at a loss before his period of incarceration. Dex bought the building, did little to repair or update the property. Yet, he was able to earn a sizable profit on short-term room rentals.

Recognizing a need in the community, he used the building for short term rentals and frequently bartered with the tenants on the terms of their stay. It was a profitable business where no one asked questions. Aponia was sure that he dealt with a special type of clientele. She wasn't sure what type of clientele was special enough to live here in filth. Then again, she and Jett were here she thought to herself.

Jett led Aponia up the dark staircase to the second floor. He stopped outside the room with the number 222 on its door. The red door stood out among the blue door to the left and the black one just down the hall with its fresher looking paint and absence of foot prints on the door. Jett used the key to open the door to a small room with a single bed on the back wall, a small scarred table at one end and a bathroom at the other. One folding chair sat next to the front door.

Aponia went to the bed and sat down. The folded stained sheets and thread bare comforter lay on the bed awaiting placement on the bed. The mattress had seen better days. Since seating options were limited, she sat down and released the pup to the floor. Aponia had so many questions as she twisted her hands in her lap deciding where to start. The pup sniffed about occasionally yapping at a dead rat in the corner and chased big brown roaches that dashed about the floor. She suspected that the roaches were the primary room occupants.

"We need to make money to afford this room," Jett pulled the chair closer to the bed where Aponia sat.

"I'm sure we can both get a job," Aponia started wanting him to know she was willing to contribute to their team effort. "In a short time, we can find a place of our own." Aponia said sharing the story of love and marriage that she had in her head. They would buy a house and have four babies that looked like Jett. They would live happily ever after.

"We need things right now," Jett explained watching her more closely. "You may be able to get us some money quickly." Aponia did not like the way Jett was watching her. His reactions reminded her of that of the lascivious man he called Dex. She was beginning to doubt the story in her head would match the reactions she was seeing in Jett's eyes.

"You could get a job quicker since you're older," Aponia proposed uncomfortably. Jett didn't answer. "What about working at the diner with your mom or at the corner store?"

"No," Jett responded. "No openings and I am too young to be legally employed there." Aponia didn't like where this conversation was going. She also didn't believe his explanation.

"How do you know?" she asked quizzing him. "We just got here. How can I make money quicker when I'm younger than you. I can't work legally either!" Jett didn't answer. "And what were the terms this Dex person talked about?" Aponia watched Jett as he fidgeted nervously in his chair. "What?"

Jett began drawing out the conversation nervously, "Dex has needs." Aponia knew she didn't like what was coming. "If you allow Dex and a few of his friends to touch you, then we would have a place to stay for a few weeks."

"NO!" she screamed. "Never!" Tears streamed down her face as her brain struggled to process the information presented by Jett. She didn't believe that he would even ask such a thing. The pup began running in circles barking at Jett. Everything in her head said it was time to go. She moved to stand, but Jett blocked her path of escape.

Jett placed his hands firmly on her shoulders pressing her back down looking into her eyes. "Yes, you will do as I say!" he stated unequivocally. "You have no choice! We have no choice!" His eyes had changed to hard orbs that she didn't recognize. This was not the Jett that had been so tender with her when they had made plans for a future together. His eyes were angry and unrelenting. Was this what the others had seen?

Aponia shook her head violently back and forth trying to dislodge his grip on her shoulders. She pulled her bag onto her shoulders, pushed past Jett and started toward the door. The pup was close on her heals. Jett grabbed Aponia by her waist raising her off her feet and tossed her back on the bed. Flailing wildly, Aponia bounced and tried to regain her footing on the floor.

Jett's face turned angry and hard. Aponia did not recognize the love of her life. In his place was an angry tyrant that was manhandling her and forcing her back onto the bed. Aponia grabbed the metal bed post at the far end of the bed and kicked at her pursuer. The pup hopped up and down avoiding Jett's feet trying to express his displeasure with his sharp teeth while defending his protector.

Jerking her violently by her feet as she hung on as if her life depended on it, Aponia's head slammed into the bedpost. Her head bounced off the bedpost loudly with a crack before hitting a second time on the side of her head. Blood gushed from a gash in her forehead and just above her ear. Her body went limp. Aponia smelled the strong coppery smell of blood and tasted it in her mouth. Her vision slowly faded into blackness. The world was closing in and she was losing her grip on the here and now. The pup barked wildly at her feet running in circles.

Jett shook Aponia's body to wake her. Nothing. "Please get up!" he yelled before grabbing his backpack and clearing out all traces of himself in the room. "Poni! Poni!" he pleaded craw fishing his way toward the door with his backpack over his shoulder. He watched the growing pool of blood around her upper body.

Taking one last look at his friend's body before grabbing the door knob, Jett turned toward the door. He had never seen so much blood in his life. Jett was not prepared to deal with the death of a friend. It had been an accident and he wanted to flee home to safety as quickly as possible. At fifteen, children weren't supposed to die right there in front of you. We were invincible or so he thought. This was not a world that he'd been exposed to. Just then, he was startled by Dex standing in the doorway with his hand up in mid knock.

Jett's face was contorted in shock and his eyes bugged out of his head. "I…I…didn't mean it!" Jett stumbled over the words as he struggled for them to come out.

Cigar clenched tightly in his teeth, Dex calmly looked into the room and back at Jett. "You were never here!" He stated sharply. "Go home and stay home. I'll take care of this."

Jett ran down the hall like his shorts were on fire. Dex calmly closed the door and pulled out a mobile phone to make an anonymous call to the police department for medical assistance. He'd made calls in the past for people that died in and around the property. He refused to leave his name and knew that his name was not registered to the phone that he held in his hand. After making the call, Dex quickly slid his feet back down the hall in his broke down slippers looking more like an abominable snow man fleeing the scene. His body twisted comically at the waist and upper body as he made his way down the hall. He didn't stop until he was safely back in his apartment.

Chapter Three

Valerie Monarch had gone into her daughter's room to close the window where she found Aponia gone. She immediately woke Sophia up to question her about the whereabouts of her sister. Groggily, Sophia rubbed her eyes trying to wake up before shaking her head no. Valerie ran from the room on short sturdy legs yelling to her son. Solomon had not seen her either. Valerie called her ex-husband, Ethan Monarch, to get help finding their daughter. He was at the house within 15 minutes dressed in jeans, a white t-shirt and tennis shoes. His day-old beard and disheveled appearance made him look uncharacteristically out of sorts. When he finally got his bearings, he began barking instructions to his wife.

"Val, call the police," Ethan instructed as he started out the door to begin searching the neighborhood. "I'll search the neighborhood and check in with Ariyana and that guy she likes." Ethan Monarch couldn't think clearly and couldn't think of her daughter's boyfriend's name. By God, he had remembered where he lived and would strangle him if he had anything to do with his daughter's disappearance. He knew he couldn't trust that kid. Making his own decision, the kid was grown at fifteen doing as he pleased. Now, he was free to do as he pleased with his daughter, Ethan thought to himself. With every step his anger grew.

Tears streamed down Valerie's cheeks as the guilt washed over her. Their earlier argument may have contributed to her daughter's flight from home. "Where did you go?" she murmured to herself as she called 911 and gave the officer their address, Aponia's full name and description. Afterward, she quizzed Solomon and Sophia for any clues that they might have on their sister's whereabouts. Neither Solomon or Sophia knew anything.

Her mother paced back and forth trying to think clearly. Nothing seemed to make sense. She vowed to get her daughter the help they had been putting off for previous bouts with misbehavior and emotional outbursts. She had become angrier and angrier generally about nothing in particular. Valerie had known her daughter's outbursts were abnormal, but she refused to believe that her daughter might be emotionally unstable in any way. If they found her, the family would be seeking help she decided. She prayed to God that her daughter would return home safely.

Three houses down on Union Boulevard, Ethan Monarch walked up the narrow concrete walkway to two steps leading to a small square porch. The white house with the green shutters was dark and the windows blended into the siding. He banged on the front door with his fist causing the sound to reverberate through the front of the house. A short time later, a disheveled male with dark curly hair opened the door wearing a white t-shirt and green and red pajama bottoms.

He grunted, "What's going on?"

"My daughter is missing?" Ethan answered franticly. "Has your daughter seen her?" A small face appeared from around her father. Her mother's head filled with pink hair curlers made her presence known as well.

"I haven't seen her since we walked home from school on Friday," Ariyana's voice croaked. "How long has she been missing?" Ethan shrugged his shoulders indicating that he didn't know and didn't know what else to say. This was not like his daughter. She was responsible even if she was occasionally emotional and impulsive. He thought to himself that he needed to stop making excuses for his daughter's angry behavior. In his heart, he knew there was a deeper problem. That problem may have put her life in danger.

"I'll come out and help look for her," Ariyana's father, Derek Rochier, said disappearing inside and reappearing with his jacket. As Ariyana started out the door, her father pushed her back into the house. "I'll be back as soon as I can. Go back to bed!" He waited to hear the locks click into place before he joined Ethan on the landing below. Together they walked toward Old Depot Road.

Next, the two men walked down one block and over to Jett's home on Confederate Way. As Ethan found his rhythm walking next to Derek, he reviewed his memory of Aponia's boyfriend and mother. Tesha Franklin had gone to school with he and his siblings. She had become pregnant in high school and eventually dropped out of school. Ethan wasn't sure of the father, but most assumed the father was incredibly irresponsible to allow her to take the blame for the pregnancy completely upon herself. Ethan thought Tesha beautiful, but a bit permissive with her son. He didn't appreciate that lifestyle for his impressionable daughter.

Derek waited as Ethan walked onto the dark wooden porch and began knocking on the front door. A living room light popped on in the window and curtains moved just adjacent to the front door. The round face of a woman peered out. No makeup on her face, Ethan easily recognized the woman as Tesha now bundled into a blue over-sized bath robe. She pushed at her hair before opening the door quinting at the man on her porch, Tesha asked, "What do you want?" As recognition lit her face, Tesha asked, "Ethan is that you?"

Ethan nodded his head yes and explained that his daughter was missing. "I have only recently returned home from work, but I'll wake Jett." She opened the door wider to allow Ethan and Derek entry into the foyer. Pulling her robe closer to her body and to avoid kicking discarded books on the floor with her bare feet, she turned on another lamp on an end table. Clothing lay in disarray on the sofa and Tesha gathered them up quickly and placed them in a clothes basket as she passed.

A few minutes later, Tesha emerged from a bedroom down the hall followed by a sleepy teen. His hair stood in uneven tufts on the top of his head as if he had been pulling at it. He was clad in baggy shorts and a green camouflage shirt. Rubbing his eyes as he struggled to wake himself, he followed his mother in his bare feet to the living area where the men waited.

"When was the last time that you saw my daughter?" Ethan asked not waiting for formal greetings. "She is missing." He wanted an excuse to lay waste to this kid. Derek placed his hand on his friend's shoulder to calm him.

"I haven't seen her," Jett answered looking from Ethan, Derek and then to his mother. "We broke up a few days ago and I've been dating Jenny." Ethan thought that may be a comforting since he didn't actually like the kid for his daughter anyway. However, he needed someone to blame for this mess. Deflated, he gave up the anger that had been directed at Jett.

"I'm sorry that we disturbed you," Ethan said genuinely hating to upset the family needlessly. "I wish we were meeting under better circumstances." Tesha nodded as the men disappeared out the front door and into the darkness. They walked back toward Derek's home. Ethan thanked Derek for his help and decided to return to Val and his children and regroup with his family.

The police had come and gone when Ethan arrived home. The police promised to be on alert for Aponia, but did not seem overly concerned with a runaway child. They said casually that they all show up eventually referring to teen runaways. This was little comfort for the Monarch family. Ethan held his wife in the dark and sent his children back to bed. Ethan slept on the sofa in the living room so that they could start searching early. They agreed to wait until morning to continue searching as a safety precaution.

Just before dawn, the Monarch household was awakened by two police officers. One had a kind round face with a large rotund belly clad in a dark blue police uniform. His name tag read Officer Bert Gleeson. The other was younger with a slender body, reddened cheeks and wearing the same uniform. His name tag read Officer Jack Coleman. Their eyes held worry and something that Ethan could not identify. He didn't want to ask the question, but he knew it wasn't good when awakened by police officers at dawn when your child was missing. The officers explained that Aponia had been found and transported to St. Francis Hospital.

"Is she ok?" Ethan asked holding his wife. The officer's eyes revealed nothing.

"We need you to go to the hospital immediately," Officer Bert Gleeson explained. "She is in serious condition."

"Where was she found? What happened!" her mother asked visibly shaken. The officers turned and motioned for them to come as soon as possible. This could not be good when the police were not willing to provide basic details. Ethan and Valerie ran from the room and began gathering their children for their journey to the hospital. Ethan drove while Valerie prayed. Solomon and Sophia looked on in shock from the back seat of Ethan's 2015 Black Honda Civic not believing this was actually happening.

As the bright red emergency room sign came into view, Ethan slowed and Valerie's praying became more fervent. Hospitals had never been welcoming in Ethan's experience. The bright lights were cold and mysterious holding both hope and pain. Along a window lined corridor, a police officer greeted and guided them to a small glass front prayer room off the waiting room. The room was cold and brightly lit holding four plastic uncomfortable chairs.

As the family anxiously awaited an explanation, the police suggested that Solomon and Sophia wait in a glass enclosure at the far end of the waiting room where a television and children's books lay on small cluttered tables. Solomon didn't want to agree, but responded to the instructions in his father's stern eyes. He and his sister left sitting across the way inside a glass enclosure behind a small table in full view of the adults.

When the parents were seated, Officer Bert Gleason explained that he and his partner responded to an anonymous call for help at a dilapidated building on Gentry Street. Aponia was found in a second-floor apartment in a pool of blood with visible head injuries. She had no identification or belongings with her except for her dog.

Ethan and Valerie looked at one another then asked simultaneously, "What dog?"

Officer Gleeson looked down at his report and back at the parents before speaking. "She was found with a small brown and white pup that looked like he'd seen a few fights." The officer motioned for his partner to bring in the pup.

Valerie spoke up first. "I don't recognize this dog." She crossed her hands over her chest. "You are clearly mistaken!" Ethan rubbed the small animal between his ears and stroked his matted fur.

"The dog barking helped us to locate your daughter quickly. The anonymous caller didn't mention which apartment on the second floor that he'd heard yelling and barking come from. We were unable to get an answer when we tried to call the person back for additional information. Luckily, there were a limited number of apartments on the second floor." The officer looked exasperated. "If the dog's not yours, we can turn it over to the animal shelter."

"What will happen to it?" Valerie asked curiously. Ethan took the pup from the officer and cuddled him into his chest.

"I suspect if no one claims him or adopts him, he will be euthanized," The officer explained as a matter of fact.

Ethan rubbed the little pup under his chin and made him coo in ecstasy. "We will hang on to him until his owner is found." Ethan looked at Valerie for confirmation. She nodded her head in agreement.

Officer Gleeson resumed his verbal report. The pup's barking alerted officers to a problem. Aponia Monarch was found shortly afterward. Medical assistance was called and she was transported to the hospital. A canvass of the apartment building found no one that saw her come into the building or knew how she got there. Crying softly, Valerie and Ethan listened as Officer Gleeson shared what had happened. Afterward, they prepared themselves emotionally to see their daughter. Solomon was instructed to stay inside the glass enclosure with his sister and the pup. Recognizing the importance of the hour, Solomon held all questions and promised to keep his sister and the pup safe.

Following the officers, Ethan and Valerie were led through automated double doors and into a brightly lit medical suite. The suites were divided into many smaller glass enclosures with curtains along the outer walls providing privacy for its occupants. A nurse sat behind a horse shoe shaped desk with charts, papers and other equipment in a central area outside the enclosures.

The group was directed to room seven. A small twin bed sat underneath a large silver domed light. Dangerous pointy surgical instruments were laid out on the counter along one wall and a steel mobile rolling table stood next to the bed. A television craned from the opposite wall with the sound muted. No one seemed interested in what was playing on the television. The air smelled of medicinal cleaning products.

Pale and lifeless, Aponia lay in the bed covered by a white sheet pulled up to her neck. Her round glasses lay on the rolling table next to the bed. Valerie and Ethan looked down at their daughter whose head was heavily bandaged in white gauze. Tears continued down their cheeks as they willed strength into their daughter's body. For her own safety, Aponia had been placed in a drug induced comma to allow her body to heal. Time seemed to stand still.

"This could not be happening, could it?" Valerie thought to herself. She agreed to take the first watch with Aponia while Ethan sat in the emergency room lounge with his other children. While their parents were away, Solomon and Sophia took to calling the pup Rowdy. The feisty little mop demanded attention and would not be denied.

Valerie continued to pray by her daughter's bedside as the strong antiseptic smells surrounded them. This was not the way she had anticipated starting her day, but her daughter was alive and fighting for her life. That was something to be thankful for.

For several days, life for the Monarch family revolved around daily visits to the hospital. Aponia's face had taken on more color in her cheeks with time. Solomon and Sophia visited Aponia's bedside hoping to see their sister wake from her long slumber. Rowdy had become a part of the family.

In case an owner was found, Ethan left his contact information with the police department and animal shelter. Gone was Rowdy's matted bristly fur and food insecurity. He'd come to trust that his new family would provide for him and feed him regularly. Ethan purchased a small square bed that looked like a big pillow with raised sides. His raised food and water bowl was regularly filled. In a short time, Rowdy was fitting into his family like he'd always been there. However, he occasionally whined for the one member that he had not been allowed to see…the little girl that he'd tried to protect.

Valerie continued to sit quietly praying at her baby's bedside willing her eyes to open. Ethan took responsibility for transporting children to school, hospital, and other school functions as needed. They were becoming a well-oiled machine.

Chapter Four

When Aponia's eyes fluttered open, she saw the watery form of a man. She blinked several times to clear the remaining cobwebs from her mind. She was in a room that smelled of antiseptics and cleaning solutions. She lay on a small twin sized bed under a white sheet surrounded by stainless steel tools lining the cabinets and a small rolling table next to the bed. The surfaces were covered with syringes, gauze and other first aid supplies. The air in the room was cold and unmoving.

Aponia awoke to a smooth brown face covered with a thick black mustache and beard wearing a tattered blue uniform jacket with tarnished gold trim and medium gray pants standing across from her. She tried desperately to focus on the face and her surroundings. Nothing seemed normal. The military uniform was not one that she recognized, but it looked old, worn and stained with a mixture of blood, mud and things that she couldn't identify. The dull blue eyes in the brown face watching her appeared to look deep within her soul to a place that she often tried to avoid. The intense scrutiny proved unnerving.

"Who are you?" she asked when her curiosity got the best of her. The man smiled understandingly patting her arm through the white sheet covering her body. Aponia looked down at herself and then at her surroundings. The light from the overhead lamp was intense and the sterile environment reminded her of a hospital. Had she been taken to a hospital? If so, why was there no pain? How had she gotten here? Where was Jett? She closed her eyes trying to reconstruct what had happened to her. "Am I dead?" she asked not really wanting the answer.

The deep voice of the military man finally spoke, "No. You are not dead. My name is William Green, but you may call me Mr. Billy. Most young people do."

"Why am I here Mr. Billy?" Aponia raised to her elbows from a reclining position moving the bright white sheets from around her upper body. "How did I get here?"

The figure stood in the light creating a bright yellow silhouette causing him to look like an apparition in the brightly lit room. He moved slowly around the room never taking his eyes off of her, but the silhouette surrounding him never shifted as his position changed creating a ghostly glow.

"Mr. Billy, are you going to hurt me?" she asked lying prostrate on the table again bracing for the answer. It crossed her mind that her bad behavior had finally caught up with her and she was going down there to the place where her mother had forbidden her to say out loud. "Am I down you know where?"

"Of course not," Mr. Billy smiled. "I simply want to share my story with you." She was very confused. Why did she feel like a prisoner unable to escape from this man and his "story". Aponia was not totally convinced that her behavior had finally earned her a one-way slide to the nether world.

"Where is my family?" Aponia asked feeling scared of what Mr. Billy's story held for her.

"They are safe." Mr. Billy pulled a stainless-steel stool away from the far wall and sat next to Aponia's head. Fearfully, Aponia gulped loudly and looked once more into the blue eyes watching her.

"I served my country in the Civil War," he began.

Eyes widened to orbs that nearly popped from Aponia's sockets. "The Civil War was fought more than 160 years ago! Are you dead? Are you sure that I am not dead?"

"Look there." He motioned for Aponia to look toward the wall farthest from their position. He raised his scarred arms extending from the uniform sleeves. Gesturing slowly toward the opposite wall with his palms face up, light emanated from his fingertips.

As she watched, the wall silently fell away revealing green prairie grass, a cloudy overcast sky, and a dreary misty rain. The air smelled of gun powder and sweat. Aponia could taste the coppery taste of blood in her mouth. Gun fire sounded rhythmically in the distance. Bodies of the dead and dying soldiers were littered all about. Blood spattered uniforms, bodies, the grounds, trees and everything in between. The scene was overwhelming for her.

Aponia's head slowly took in the devastation that lay before her. There was a heaviness in her body as she tried to process this information. "The date was July 17, 1863," Mr. Billy said locking from Aponia to the scene revealed before them. Aponia couldn't speak as the fear moved from her head to her feet paralyzing her in place.

"I was an escaped slave from Arkansas," he spoke from somewhere far away. Aponia couldn't reconcile what she learned about the Civil War from history books compared to what Mr. Billy was saying. He continued, "My wife and six children were also runaway slaves from Arkansas during the chaos of the Civil War. My beautiful Hattie blessed me with four strong boys and two smart girls." Mr. Billy wanted to keep them safe.

The southern slave owners did not want slavery to end because they were receiving free labor on their farms ensuring future profits. For several generations Mr. Billy's family had been enslaved in Arkansas, South Carolina and Florida. Since his family was part of that free labor, they were not in favor or continuing as slaves. When they saw an opportunity, they along with other enslaved ran. This was their opportunity to escape bondage.

"I don't remember reading about enslaved people serving in the military during the Civil War," Aponia commented as she took in the devastation.

Mr. Billy explained, "History depends on who is telling the story. Most slaves were unable to read or write. Those that did didn't always have access to writing their stories down or recording it for future generations. Eventually there were African American newspapers, but distribution was limited." Aponia nodded her head acknowledging that she heard and understood.

Mr. Billy smiled. After escaping, Mr. Billy and his family walked all night and hid themselves during the day. Food consisted of whatever they could find in the area where they hid. Both he and his wife carried the youngest of their children trying to move as swiftly as possible. His family made their way to a small all-black community that was later to become Summit, Oklahoma, when the Civil War threw their new life into chaos.

Indian Territory, which became the state of Oklahoma in 1907, was a safe haven among enslaved people because there was no jurisdiction among law enforcement officers. Native Americans had been forced to relocate to Indian Territory by the government. Many outlaws populated this area because they felt they were safe from the long arm of the law. Native Americans living in the areas were restricted to enforcing laws only within the tribes. However, the slave's way of life was threatened with the Civil War encroaching into Indian Territory.

Formerly enslaved people fought on both sides of the war. Some voluntarily fought while others chose to move further north to freedom; however, some enslaved were forced to fight with their slave owners or face death. As for the Monarch family, Mr. Billy chose to fight voluntarily for the Union to give his family a chance to maintain freedom for his children.

"On January 13, 1863, I left my family and joined with other formerly enslaved people or freedmen in the First Kansas Colored Volunteer Regiment to fight with the Union troops against the Confederate Army. The soldiers in the regiment were committed to one another to support one another and to protect us from soldiers who thought them less than other soldiers. I did not want my children to have to endure slavery any longer. I had to fight for them," Mr. Billy pleaded for understanding.

Aponia had never experienced slavery or heard much about it among her family. Although her knowledge was limited regarding slavery, she had never talked to anyone who had lived through it or had close relatives who had. Seeing no other option to his family remaining free, Mr. Billy made the decision to fight.

Honey Springs had been a supply depot and was critical for maintaining freedom in Indian Territory. Mr. Billy fought with his best friend, Avery Markham, who was an escaped slave from Missouri. Together, they watched each other's back during the fight. Before the war, Honey Springs had been part of Indian Territory, where Native Americans had been forced to live following the Trail of Tears, a forced displacement of more than 60,000 Native American people by the U.S. Government between 1830 and 1850. Native Americans and many emancipated or escaped slaves seeking freedom called the area home. Because the area had also operated as a supply depot for soldiers, the area became pivotal to the war and control of resources and transportation through the area.

"On July 17, 1863, Major General James G. Blunt was the Union Commander at Honey Springs," he continued pointing to the regal man in the blue and gray military union sitting atop a black war horse. "The First Kansas was an all-black freedmen regiment. It was the fourth black regiment to officially enter federal service. We were a proud group of soldiers. However, we were not treated like other races of soldiers. We were given food, clothing and weapons leftover from others. I fought, like many other volunteer soldiers, for my family's future even if things were not fair. To create a new future for my family, I proudly fought."

Aponia watched as the rows of black military men lined up gun in hand to defend the earth where they stood as ordered by their commander. Many were down on one knee defending their position as the volley of gun fire surrounded them. Red and yellow flashes followed by gray and black smoke rose in the sky. Bodies fell accompanied by shouts and screams of agony in the field before them. Tears trickled down Mr. Billy's cheeks as he watched. Aponia looked at the visibly moved man and her heart ached for him. He didn't have a choice to fight in a war that threatened to place he and his family back within the shackles of slavery. Mr. Billy had been desperate to save the next generation from the manacles of bondage.

"The death was overwhelming in the dreary mist and muck of that day. Although it felt like eternity, the battle lasted only four hours. Men that were laughing and joking hours before at the start of the day lay dead with parts of their bodies missing. Many who were injured suffered physical and mental injuries that would follow them into the next generations." Aponia did not understand how fighting today would impact future generations. Surely, the war did not continue on to future generations who had not experienced war. She feared interrupting his story and prolonging his reason for his sharing it.

"When the fighting ended and the Confederate soldiers retreated, I fell to my knees in the mud just feet away from the bodies of the dead and injured crying like a babe," Mr. Billy gazed into his past speaking just above a whisper. He was lost to his own grief. Aponia leaned over trying to hear better. "I survived and my children had a chance to live free although the Civil War continued being fought in other regions. For that day, we won and my children could continue to taste the sweet nectar of freedom." He shook his head back and forth freeing himself from the past. He blinked several times to see Aponia more clearly.

"How do you know me?" Aponia asked looking at Mr. Billy more closely. He was somehow familiar, but not. "Why are you sharing your story with me?"

"You and your family are very special to me," he stated watching her reaction. Aponia was suspicious of his use of you and your family. He smiled anticipating her question, "No, you're not dying. And no, you're not dead either."

Aponia didn't understand all the long-term implications of war. She didn't know how the Battle of Honey Springs was tied to her family. Why did he feel so compelled to share his story with her? Was her family member, the man he called his best friend, some relation to her family? Obviously, Mr. Billy had to be deceased if he served in the Battle of Honey Springs more than 160 years ago. How did he connect with her? This was such a confusing mystery that was beginning to overwhelm her senses.

"Where were her parents?" Aponia thought to herself. "Why hadn't any doctors come to talk to her?"

Aponia did not want to believe Mr. Billy. She woke up in a place that she did not ever remember being taken to. He was sharing a story that happened over 160 years ago involving people that she did not know. She muttered, "I don't understand and I don't believe you. I must be dying." For the moment, fear fell away and darkness retook her body. She was silent in the blessed darkness without death, fear, or any of the trauma that Mr. Billy had shared.

When she awoke a short time later, she was greeted once more by the solemn face of Mr. Billy. She had hoped story time was over, but apparently, it was to continue. Mr. Billy patted her arm once more, "You needed a break from the traumas of war." Aponia agreed raising herself to better see her surroundings. She was sure that the stark white sheets and stainless-steel tools indicated that she was in a hospital of some kind.

Mr. Billy pulled up the metal stool and adjusted its height to be more comfortable. His blue eyes captured her green ones before nodding his head indicating that she should watch again. He moved his big scarred hands toward the opposite wall where light emanated from his fingers and the landscape changed.

The green grass and rolling hills were littered with blood, human remains, animal carcasses, guns, batons and other remnants of war. Soldiers moved slowly gathering the injured and assessing the conditions of their comrades. There was no laughter or joy even though the Union Army had won the battle. Some soldiers sat transfixed to the landscape in shock. They had to be helped to their feet or carried away on makeshift stretchers.

After the battle ended, the earth was quiet. Leaders regrouped to assess casualties and Major General James Blunt addressed the First Kansas Regiment. The Union Commander commended the regiment for fighting like veterans preserving their line unbroken throughout the engagement. Major General Blunt stated, "The regiment's coolness and bravery in battle had never been surpassed!" The regiment had reason to cheer and they did in that moment. They celebrated as men of war who had stood, fought, and survived. Major General James Blunt promised that the details of the victory and courage would be notated in a report for all to see.

For a short time, there would be a hiatus in fighting and the soldiers returned to their families. Unfortunately, there were other battles to fight for the men of the First Kansas Regiment. The First Kansas Colored Volunteer Regiment was transitioned to the 29th U.S. Colored Infantry in April 1864 fighting with conspicuous bravery in Missouri, Indian Territory, Kansas and Arkansas.

Enslaved people were emancipated in Texas on June 19, 1865, and Mr. Billy returned home with honor and pride for his meritorious service. However, he returned home without fanfare. The regiment was formally dismantled in November 1865. Although slavery ended, emancipated slaves were unable to escape the stigma of slavery where they were considered only being a fraction of a person within the ranks of society.

Although the war ended, the remnants of battle left Mr. Billy unsettled and distraught. His nights were plagued with memories of death all around him over and over like a black and white film that never ended. For years following battle, Mr. Billy found himself easily enraged by the simplest confrontations or missteps by his wife and children.

Eventually, his wife and children began avoiding contact with him. Mr. Billy loved his family, but did not know how to turn off the war in his head. There was no one there who understood that war continued for him inside, heart and body. He smelled the gun powder, the coppery taste of blood was in his mouth, and the feelings of chaos and fear churned inside him day and night. The feelings grew more, and more, and more until he couldn't distinguish where the battle ended and his life with his family began. War was hell and the price was high.

Mr. Billy served admirably for his country, but he was left with the ravages of war. His wife came to refer to his outbursts as "the rage". Mr. Billy didn't know where the anger and rage came from inside him. Things could be perfectly normal and then, something triggered him to anger. He only knew that after the war he felt guilty because he was forced to kill people that he didn't know and didn't know him.

Both sides of the battle fought for a cause and lives were changed because of it. The anger seemed to begin deep in his soul and gradually rise to the surface in a red-hot flash bursting into outbursts with his wife, children, neighbors and any other unfortunate person who crossed his path. The rage was usually disproportionate to the perceived misdeed. Mr. Billy came to believe that he deliberately waited for something to happen as an excuse to release the pressure of the rage deep inside him. In any case, he knew it was not fair to the people he loved. He accepted that he returned from war a broken man.

Mr. Billy turned to Aponia and motioned her to look at the scenery as it changed. Gone were the dead bodies and signs of war. In its place were fields of brown and green stringy prairie grass punctuated by large trees and a creek to the west. This is where Mr. Billy went to escape the dreams and memories of battle. He sat on the creek's edge next to a large oak tree with his back to Aponia with his feet dangling in the water. She had come to recognize Mr. Billy's form although they have not known each other before now. Back and forth, he swung his feet.

In his hand, he held a smooth blue, green stone rubbing it back and forth with his big thumb. She could just make out the colors and shape. This was his calming stone or distraction device. This became a focal point to transfer energy from his body to the stone. The stone winked in his hand like it was grabbing her attention and saying hello. She knew the stone was significant, but wasn't sure why.

Sadly, his family had had enough of Mr. Billy's rage and outbursts after ten years. His wife, Hattie, feared for her safety and escaped into the night with her children leaving no forwarding address. The next morning, he awoke to an eerily quiet home. It was not as if he had not expected it at some point. He'd just hoped that the day wouldn't come.

Nevertheless, Mr. Billy was devastated blaming himself for his outbursts and the fear that he evoked in his wife and children. Their leaving brought about a cycle of depression and more rage at what he had caused his family. Mr. Billy vowed to restore what had been stolen from his family and would not rest until his mission was complete.

Aponia asked cautiously, "Why are you telling me all this?" She rose up on her elbows to look more closely at the man so intent on telling his story. His blue eyes glowed. "I've never seen a black man with blue eyes," she voiced her observation as she continued to look into his now sparkling eyes.

"I am telling you this to help me rest peacefully and for future generations." Aponia looked at him puzzled and then lay back trying to take in this new information. "It is my hope that you learn that you are not alone. Freedom is available to you if you choose it."

"You say that I am not dead, but I am most certain that you are," Aponia stated unequivocally. "Are you saying that I can help bring you rest and peace. Do you even know who I am? Why me?" In response, Mr. Billy continued with his story.

After his family disappeared, Mr. Billy began looking for his family in the all-black settlements in Indian Territory. William "Little Billy" Green was Mr. Billy's youngest son. Little Billy and his wife, Harriet, were living in Red Bird, Oklahoma, by then with children of their own. Unlike his siblings, Little Billy had exhibited a rage similar to his father.

This was a puzzle because Little Billy had never experienced the ravages of war. The anger was intense and he exhibited behavioral outburst like his father. Mr. Billy had hoped his sacrifice would create a better life for his family. Little Billy was not been forced to fight in the war, but he carried with him a rage that Mr. Billy had experienced first-hand.

Mr. Billy knew he was the source of his son's anger and was unsure how to make things better for him. At that time, Mr. Billy wasn't sure how to make things better for himself. He had returned from battle ill-equipped to deal with the aftermath of the death and destruction of war. Little Billy did not know how to deal with his anger and the pain of losing his father. While Mr. Billy was physically in his son's life, he was emotionally absent caught in a horrible world inside himself.

Although he readily admitted to not being a good father, Mr. Billy failed to accept responsibility for screaming at them. Simple things like losing their school books, dropping food on the floor, or simply forgetting to do their chores resulted in angry tirades. He was not intentionally unkind, but he was.

As he grew older, Mr. Billy was befriended by other freedmen soldiers that shared similar experiences. He learned that he was not alone and that others could ease the burden. Together, they helped each other deal with the war, accept responsibility for their actions, and make plans for a better future. It was not until Mr. Billy was on his death bed that he realized he would not be able to live long enough to ask for his family's forgiveness. Little Billy had sought alcohol to calm the rage. It only offered a long, protracted death where his family were forced to watch helplessly as he destroyed himself.

Mr. Billy's death did not offer comfort from his chaotic life, there was no rest for him. He had committed to warning those that came after him that they had to seek help for the rage. This curse did not end with Little Billy, it was passed to Little Billy's middle son, Arthur. When Arthur was young, family assumed that he was a strong-willed child that had behavioral problems. It was not until he was an adult married to Betsy that his rage overwhelmed his life. Like his father and grandfather, Arthur abused his wife verbally and threatened his children when they made minor missteps.

Once when Arthur's son, Fred, failed to make a perfect score on a test, he was greeted with screams of disappointment from his father. Fred's grade reflected an average score for his class and he admitted that he had done his very best. Psychologically, Fred began to think of himself as unworthy of love. The handsome young man with a quick wit was unable to recognize his positive attributes in the mirror. The bulky young man with dark hair, hazel eyes and a gifted singing voice was unable to realize his value to his family and community. He drifted into alcohol abuse and away from his family and friends. Fred was mentally lost to his wife, children and grandchildren, though his body was never far from them. Mr. Billy's effort to change the trajectory of their lives were unsuccessful.

Unfortunately, this was not the end of the rage. Fred's second oldest son, Alex Green, was afflicted similarly. He too sought peace in the arms of alcohol. Alex's daughter, Kittie, inherited the rage in adulthood, but tried hard not to succumb to alcohol as her forebears had. The tall willowy framed woman with the pleasant smile and eloquent words struggled as well. Although she tried many therapies suggested by her elders, nothing seemed to work.

She tried positive thinking, natural remedies including St. John's Wort, rose tea, and lemon balm, as well as denying the existence of the rage. In the end, her life was cut short from the affliction. Her husband and children paid a heavy price for the rage and ravages of war although she never served a day in her life. Mr. Billy cried for those that he was unable to help. However, he would never give up until he restored what the war had taken away.

Taking pity on Aponia's confused state, Mr. Billy sat and explained, "First, I have blue eyes because of my mixed heritage. My father was a slave owner who had blue eyes. You cannot always tell what lies within by looking from the outside, Poni." She was shocked at his use of her nickname which was only used by her family. What did he know that he wasn't telling her?

"However, you can sometimes understand more fully by looking at the obvious. You must pay attention." Confusion showed on Aponia's face. She didn't know how to respond and didn't understand the significance of the simple statement. Mr. Billy changed the subject moving in a different direction with a question. "Did you know that you were born with your umbilical cord around your neck and butterfly wings on your left shoulder?" Now she was intrigued. How would he know that?

"I've never heard that!" Aponia jumped to a sitting position. "You could be lying to me to gain my trust. That's not going to work with me! You don't know me! You're dead!"

He patted her hand soothing her fears. "Ask your mother."

"How do you know my mother?" Aponia demanded.

"In due time, you will understand all," he smiled. "Remember this, the rage will live until you learn to quit feeding it." Then he was gone.

Aponia sat partially covered in this cold hospital room not understanding anything. At this point, she wasn't sure that she hadn't just gone crazy. "Come back Mr. Billy," she said quietly calling to him. "I have more questions." No response. In time, she lay back down in the bed, pulled the sheet up to her chin and rested in the blackness that soon enveloped her.

Chapter Five

Aponia awoke with the white sheet covering her body to her chin and tucked securely under her body. She looked around the all too familiar room. It had been the same when Mr. Billy shared his story. But was it real she thought? The medicinal smell surrounded her and the bright light blinded her. The face of her mother moved toward her as the light behind her created a glow outlining her head and shoulders. Aponia's vision was still blurry, but she recognized the soft flowery fragrance of her mother and her mother's voice cut through the haze.

"Finally," her mother squeezed her hand in relief patting the side of her face tenderly. "You were asleep so long that we were beginning to worry that you may never wake up." Her father's familiar face floated into her field of vision. He was smiling and crying at the same time. Aponia tried to remember the last time that she'd seen her father cry. Nothing came to mind.

"Where is Mr. Billy?" Aponia asked a little confused searching the room for his familiar uniform and blue eyes.

Her parents looked at one another and then around the room. Valerie Monarch asked, "Who is Mr. Billy?"

"He was in the Battle of Honey Springs and he told me about his family," Aponia explained. "He said that I was born with my "um... um...bilicard" around my neck."

Valerie and Ethan looked at each other confused. "How did you know that?" Valerie finally asked.

"Mr. Billy told me that," she pleaded for understanding. "He was here in this room with me."

Ethan looked at his daughter rubbing her arm trying to comfort her. "Me and your mother have been here since you've been here and there haven't been anyone visiting you by the name of Mr. Billy. We would have seen him."

Aponia closed her eyes tightly and shook her head. "What happened to me? Did I die?" she asked beginning to cry. Her mother hugged her raising her upper body clear of the small bed. Her father put his arms around them both. All cried together. They were happy that she was alive.

"Poni, you are very much alive and we are thankful for you," Ethan commented squeezing his wife and daughter. "Would you like to see Solomon and Sophia?" No, Aponia didn't want to Solomon and Sophia. Not right now when she was so confused. She wanted to know who Mr. Billy was and why he had shared his story with her. Her mother stroked Aponia's cheek lovingly as she'd done so many times before to calm her nerves. Ethan left the room to retrieve her sister and brother.

A few minutes later, Sophia burst into the small room followed by her brother. Eyes red, Solomon looked like he'd been crying although Aponia was sure he'd never admit it. Sophia was another story.

"Welcome, back!" Sophia ran in and held her arms up for her father to lift her to see her sister better. "Dad said that I wasn't to ask too many questions because your head was all twisted up. Are your brains all twisted?" Sophia leaned forward to see if it was true for herself. Ethan exchanged a look of exasperation with his wife and son.

"Brat, I am sure dad wanted you to keep that part to yourself," Solomon frowned at his chatty little sister who was batting her beautiful green eyes innocently.

Sophia looked to her father who frowned looking very similar to his son. She shrugged her shoulders and commented, "You got to express yourself more clearly, daddy." Ethan laughed at his daughter's candor and similar words used by Valerie. Sophia who was known for saying what she was not supposed to say simply smiled her most mischievous smile reducing her father to laughter. Sophia knew how to work a crowd, which generally kept her out of trouble especially with her father.

"I wonder where you heard that?" Ethan asked his daughter as he looked conspiratorially at Valerie. Sophia looked to her mother as if to say "duhh".

"I may have said it on occasion," Valerie smiled avoiding Ethan's glare. They both dissolved into laughter that proved contagious and all joined in the fun.

Solomon moved closer to his little sister and touched her arm. He was glad that his mouthy little sister had survived. He had prayed that God would save Aponia. In the past week, he had prayed more than he'd ever prayed in his life. Regardless of their disagreements in the past, he wanted Aponia to live and return home to the family safely. He didn't care if her brains were scrambled. She was his sister and he vowed to protect her.

Enjoying her family's warmth, Aponia still had questions. Was she crazy? Did she really see Mr. Billy? Aponia pinched herself leaving a red welt on her skin. If this was a dream, she wanted to wake up now.

"Why did you do that?" her mother asked quietly.

"I wanted to make sure that I was awake."

Valerie smiled at her daughter understanding that the comma had left her in a confused state. All would be right in time Aporia thought to herself.

The days flew by in the hospital and Aponia gained her strength. Within four days, the doctor released Aponia to go home. She knew things had changed when she was ushered into their small living room with the plastic covered sofa underneath the plate glass window at the front of the house. A smaller tan love seat was flanked by two chocolate wing-backed chairs. A glass coffee table sat unused in front of the sofa save for a clear glass vase filled with spring flowers of red, yellow, green, blue and pink. Aponia had missed the fragrance of cinnamon and flowers that permeated all the rooms of the house.

There was a new family member that Aponia wanted to reacquaint herself with. She heard in the hospital that the pup had been found with her and the family adopted him. The brown and white pup that looked to be well fed and full of energy bounded out of the kitchen. He yapped at her feet and stretched himself up against her leg begging for attention. Aponia picked the pup up and cuddled him into her arms. He squirmed and pawed happily at his girl.

Saying his name experimentally, Aponia repeated the name Rowdy several times to see if it fit. She finally judged it a good fit when he cooed in response. "I've missed you boy," she cuddled him close. "You tried to save me." Rowdy licked her face energetically.

Aponia walked around the house with the pup in her arms reorienting herself to her surroundings. The house smelled of the familiar cinnamon that her mother used in cookies. The small house was home. The kitchen still had the small wooden table with four metal chairs surrounding it. The white counter tops were clean and held only the essential spices of salt, pepper, sugar, cinnamon and thyme. The refrigerator and stove sat at the far end of the kitchen while the sink sat underneath the window opposite the table. Yes, she was home.

Next, she walked through the living area and down the hall to where the bedrooms lay. She and Sophia shared a room on the left side of the hallway. She opened the door and found her bed neatly made with her pillow and Mulan comforter. Sophia's bed was covered with a pink comforter and matching pillow. Solomon's room was next door and her mother's room across the hall. Things were just as she remembered.

When she returned to the living room, her mother pulled her onto the sofa next to her. Ethan sat across from her. Solomon sensed something was amiss looking to his father for guidance. Ethan motioned with his head for Solomon to continue to the kitchen and take his youngest sister with him. Sophia was oblivious to her father's motion as she happily chatted with Honey, their tan and white striped cat, who occasionally allowed her humans to share her domain. Ethan had purchased the eight-week-old kitten for his children several months ago.

As she had grown, Honey came to believe that the humans in the home were there strictly for her pleasure and service. To say she was spoiled was an understatement. Honey hissed if she didn't feel like being touched, turned her food bowl over if she didn't like what she was being served and disappeared if humans were getting on her nerves. This was frequently the case with the chatty Sophia.

It took several days, but she was agreeable to sharing her domain with Rowdy. Honey had taught Rowdy with her claws that she was Queen Bee and that he needed to understand the hierarchy of the house. Rowdy sniffed at the ornery cat and accepted his position in the household. He seemed glad to have a home and humans to do his bidding.

Solomon pulled Sophia by her arm towing her into the kitchen and out of the sight of his parents. Aponia was beginning to get the impression that something was going on as she looked between her mother and father.

"What's going on?" she asked expectantly putting Rowdy on his feet next to the sofa.

"We need to talk about some things," her mother began. "We hadn't pressed you before now about what happened and where we go from here." She let the conversation lag for emphasis. "We now need to talk about what happened."

"What do you want to know?"

"Why did you run away?" Ethan asked joining hands with Valerie for support.

Aponia breathed deeply trying to get her bearings again. "I ran away to escape the chaos of the anger and rage. It just never ends. I feel like my head is full of stuff and its spinning." Valerie didn't comprehend the magnitude of what her daughter said, but held her hand transferring the positive energy that she needed. "I just didn't want to keep fighting with everyone here."

Ethan watched refraining from asking too many questions at once. Valerie pulled her daughter close.

"Everything is not clear yet, but my memory is gradually coming back."

"How did you get to the building where you were found?" Ethan asked not sure if he wanted the answer.

"Jett and I walked there," Aponia answered sheepishly. Her parents looking between one another confused. "What?" she asked when they didn't seem to believe her.

Ethan started watching his daughter more closely for distress and explained that he'd spoken to Jett and his mother on the night she ran away. He shared Jett's comments that he had not seen her and that he had started dating another girl a few days before. Aponia was silent. "You have to be honest with us, Poni!" Ethan pleaded with his daughter. "We love you and want to help."

"I'm telling you the truth. Jett and I had talked about running away, getting married and having a family one day."

Anger began to creep into Ethan as his cheeks reddened. He didn't speak. Valerie stepped in as the voice of reason, "Poni, you may be a little confused. You talked about a Mr. Billy when you woke up. Now you say Jett took you to that place. Things may be a little confused in your head."

Aponia cried, "Ask Mr. Dex on the first floor of the building and he will tell you about me and Jett. Why won't you believe me?"

Ethan calmed himself and agreed to go by the building and see if he could find a Mr. Dex on the first floor of the building. Aponia went to her room a short time later questioning what she believed. She wasn't sure what was real and what was fantasy at this point.

Ethan drove his Black Honda Civic to the building on Gentry Street. Four young men with baggy pants, wife beater t-shirts, and boisterous attitudes stood near the corner. They seemed to be heckling an elderly woman carrying her groceries down the sidewalk. Ethan was reluctant to become distracted from his main purpose of being in this neighborhood.

It seemed most residents were living in the neighborhood because they had few other options. Rent was cheap, poverty was overwhelming and no one asked questions about how one made a living. Ethan was watchful and wanted to maintain his own safety. He'd wished he could help more of the residents who were trapped and could not afford to find better housing. The woman being heckled finally disappeared inside a building on the next block.

Locking his car doors and pulling the handle to reassure himself it was locked, he started toward the building. He pulled the creaky door of the building open. Looking around the hallway he began knocking on random doors. No one answered. He came to a door with the number 122 on the outside. The door opened a crack at his knock and a red eyed male peered out of a dark mocha colored face. "What do you want?" asked a gruff voice.

"I'm looking for Mr. Dex," Ethan stated.

"You got him," came the reply. "Who's asking? What do you want?"

"My daughter was found here in a pool of blood on the second floor," Ethan explained. "She said you saw her here with Jett."

"She is mistaken," the voice said slamming the door in Ethan's face. He stood for a time unsure whether he actually believed him. The man made it clear that he was not willing to talk to him further.

Ethan turned around to leave startled by the rude response. When he opened the door of the building, he found a stocky boy about sixteen-years-old with an oversized t-shirt and jean shorts sitting on his car. Ethan stopped in his tracks assessing the scene and the three other guys loitering nearby who had been on the corner earlier.

"You owe me $10 for watching your car," the boy grinned widely with dark yellow teeth. Ethan watched the boy and noted the location of the others. "My friends think that would be a fair price." The others now stood with their full attention directed on Ethan.

Pulling a $5 bill from his pocket, Ethan handed the kid the money, pushed past him pulling his door open and getting into his car. He locked the door.

"You're short," the kid cocked his head to the side grinning mischievously and leaning on the car for emphasis.

Ethan turned his ignition starting the car's engine. Two of the men stood just in front of his car. Ethan yelled to the boy, "You have what I've got. Get out of my way or prepare to be run over!" Ethan gunned the engine as the two men jumped from the front of his car. The boy leaning on the car banged on the side of the car with his fists as he drove away. Ethan was angrier than he was afraid. However, he recognized that the odds were not balanced in his favor. He'd live to fight another day.

Something didn't make much sense to him. It was clear that Aponia was confused about much of the things that happened, but how did she know that the man's name was Mr. Dex? Maybe she had heard someone say his name the day she came to the building. He would think more about it later. His little girl needed him.

Ethan returned home. He and his wife again spoke with Aponia. As she sat on the side of her bed, Ethan shared the results of his meeting with Mr. Dex.

"I don't understand why he would lie," Aponia said more to herself than her parents.

"Maybe he isn't lying," Valerie offered. "Maybe you're still a little confused."

"But how would Aponia know Mr. Dex's name?" Ethan asked Valerie. "Poni, what does Mr. Dex look like?"

"He is a big black guy with a big belly and short legs," Aponia explained. "He was in apartment number 122."

Ethan's face went slack and he commented, "Mr. Dex was in apartment number 122." This revelation caused Ethan to sit back and rethink what he considered the truth. Valerie watched as he watched their daughter. "Could it be that what they thought was true wasn't?" Valerie thought to herself. Aponia watched the faces of her parents and understood they were shifting their positions.

"Why did you run away, Poni?" Ethan asked again wanting to confront the things that mattered most to him.

She didn't answer immediately. "I get so angry and I'm not sure why. Mom thinks that I am a drama queen. I don't understand why I get so angry, but I can feel it when it starts. I'm not crazy!" Aponia looked at her parents' faces and knew they didn't understand. She could see it in their faces. She was beginning to think maybe she was the crazy one. They needed help with this situation.

"Loki's mother suggested that we call a therapist to work with you," Valerie offered suggestively. "She could help you work through the anger and the confusion."

Aponia felt like she was about to explode! "I keep telling you that I'm not crazy! I don't need to talk to anyone about this!" She threw herself on the bed and put a pillow over her head pretending not to hear anything. Although Aponia wasn't sure if she needed it, she didn't want to start with some therapist.

"You're scheduled to start with a therapist tomorrow," Ethan stated forcefully. "You're not crazy, but this family needs help. You're going!"

"I'm not going!" She didn't remove the pillow from her face causing her voice to sound muffled. "I'm not!" Inside, she knew that she had to go. Something that Mr. Billy said pricked her memory and felt right although she did not want to go to any therapist that didn't know her or her situation.

"You are scheduled for your first appointment tomorrow at 2:00pm," Ethan announced before leaving the room. Closing the door behind him, Ethan's voice continued to echo in his daughter's ears.

"You will go," Valerie repeated his words. "You'll like Dr. Athena Rochier."

"I will not! I hate her already!"

Valerie continued sadly explaining," This family must get you help before you do something that gets you or someone else hurt or killed. You came very close to dying. I will not allow you to destroy yourself or anyone else." Valerie stood kissed her daughter's cheek and replaced the pillow on her face. Her footsteps became lighter and lighter as she moved to the door and disappeared into the hallway. She looked back at her daughter once more before leaving the room and closing the door quietly behind her. Aponia removed the pillow from her face and cried in earnest. She didn't want to see a therapist. She wanted to be left alone. She also wanted to talk to Jett.

Valerie and Ethan met in the living area to discuss what they'd heard. There were so many questions that came to mind.

"How could Poni know what room Mr. Dex was in and what he looked like if she hadn't met him?" Ethan began pacing back and forth in front of the plate glass window. Valerie had asked a similar question.

"I wonder if Jett knows more than what he was saying?" Ethan asked turning to his wife.

"Surely he wouldn't lie in front of his mother," Valerie commented finding it hard to believe that Jett may have taken their daughter to such a ghastly place and left her. "You don't like him anyway, so maybe you'd like that to be true?"

Ethan's face turned to a frown. "I wouldn't accuse the teen of something that I didn't think he'd done."

Not wanting to stress their amiable relationship, Valerie patted Ethan's shoulder and said genuinely, "I know you wouldn't, but it is curious. Let's focus on getting help for Poni and then deal with the rest later." She sat on the sofa and placed her face in her hands. "I've known Poni needed help for such a long time. I just didn't want to deal with it. She could have died and I refuse to ignore it anymore." Ethan joined her on the sofa and folded her into his arms. On this one, they agreed.

Aponia called Jett on her cell phone. The number rang and rang. The answering machine eventually picked up directing her to leave a message at the beep. She didn't know what to say so she hung up. Her father had told her that Jett had moved on with his new girlfriend, Jenny. She was having trouble wrapping her mind around this information. Aponia tried calling him several times more to no avail. Is something wrong with her memory? What was going on? She clearly remembered Jett asking her to allow men to touch her and then the two fighting. Although she had not shared this bit of information with her parents, it seemed so clear to her mind. This bit of information would also get Jett banned from ever talking to her by her father.

Aponia wasn't allowed to visit any of her friends except Ariyana, who confirmed that Jett was dating Jenny. Could she have been imagining things? If so, how did she get into the room at the Gentry building? How did she know about Mr. Dex and his apartment number? It was all so confusing. However, she refused to believe she was crazy. Everyone else may be crazy, but not her.

The next afternoon, Aponia's parents drove her to meet the therapist. Ethan was dressed in dark slacks and a blue collared shirt similar to his church attire. Valerie was dressed in a flowery red, yellow, and green scoop neck dress, a matching belt at her waist ending just above her knees. She looked much younger in her carefree summer attire. They waited in a small room with soft green lounge chairs lined on two walls opposite the receptionist sitting behind a sliding glass window above a tan half wall. The art on the walls was contemporary abstract paintings that featured splashes of color in the pastel colors green, pink, blue and yellow. The room seemed to exude positive energy. Aponia and her father sat as her mother checked them in.

A short time later, a small woman with thick glasses wearing a white lab coat over a stretchy black top and tiger striped yoga pants with tan Crocs on her feet greeted them. The therapist introduced herself as Dr. Athena Rochier before escorting the group into her spacious office. From behind, Dr. Rochier's hips bounced and swayed to their own internal rhythm as they pushed against the back of the lab coat.

Inside the office, four chairs surrounding a small round table sat adjacent to the door. A large brown comfy scoop chair sat in front of the massive wooden executive desk next to a small coffee table. A matching credenza sat near the back wall behind the desk with a green cushioned chair underneath. Book shelves were lined with books, assorted pictures, and other memorabilia. The carpeting was light gray creating a light airy feel to the room. The office was professional and comfortable, but Aponia had already decided that she did not like it or the therapist.

Dr. Athena Rochier was not what Aponia expected. Her smooth coffee brown face was surrounded by braids highlighted with colorful beads. She didn't look to be old enough to have become a therapist by Aponia's estimation. Her short stature dressed in a white lab coat with the stretchy garb underneath caught her attention.

She invited the Monarch family to sit at the small table next to the door. She offered each person a sampling of herbal teas. Explaining that teas often had a calming effect, she used the teas to get to know visitors better. Aponia decided to take the tea but refused to allow this eccentric person to get to know her.

Aponia selected orange tea that helped to distract her from what was to come. After she had settled into blowing the hot tea to cool it down, she returned her attention to the therapist.

The therapist began, "Aponia, what would you like me to call you?"

"Aponia Monarch," she responded folding her arms across her chest in protest. Valerie Monarch gave her daughter a stern look indicating that she was to mind her manners.

"Aponia Monarch it is," she laughed. "I like a child who knows her own mind."

Aponia's mother interjected, "We call my daughter Poni at home."

"Thank you, Ms. Monarch. I appreciate the information. Now, Aponia Monarch, what would you like me to know about you?"

Aponia looked from her mother, who was giving her the evil eye, to her father, who dared her to share a catty remark, and back to the therapist. "Nothing," Aponia finally stated.

The therapist requested that her parents trust her and the therapy process. Both looked at one another and back at their daughter daring her to embarrass them with their eyes. Valerie and Ethan were escorted to the waiting room for the remainder of the session.

Once alone, she asked Aponia to move to the brown scoop chair in front of her desk where she could be more comfortable. The therapist moved Aponia's tea to the table next to the chair before sitting behind her desk. Pulling out a file folder, she opened it and begun taking notes. Aponia watched warily with her arms crossed over her chest.

Because the silence was making her antsy, Aponia asked, "What are you writing?" the therapist put her pen down and looked back at Aponia. She asked again, "What are you writing?"

"I am completing paperwork regarding your case," she explained.

"I'm not giving you anything to write about," Aponia pouted. She was committed to making the therapist's session with her difficult and then even more difficult. If it took her days and days, she would break this lady. She had practice making life hell for her teachers, family and some friends. If she had to say so herself, she was good too.

Something caught her attention on the wall adjacent to the desk. It was a picture with of a regal Native American man with chiseled cheek bones, bronzed skin, two long black braids hanging past his shoulders, and a no-nonsense expression on his face. Just above each shoulder sat wolves, one with a passive expression and the other snarling. Underneath the picture, the caption read,

"Cherokee Proverb:

There is a battle of two wolves inside us all.

One is evil. It is anger, jealousy, greed, resentment, lies, inferiority and ego.

The other is good. It is joy, peace, love, hope, humility, kindness, empathy and truth.

The wolf that wins? The one you feed."

"What does this mean?" Aponia asked curiously pointing to the picture. Something about the picture pricked her memory of Mr. Billy's words.

Moving closer to the picture, the therapist explained, "The picture says that we all have two sides of ourselves, both good and evil. Who we are and who we become depends on which path you choose. Your life; your choice. If you choose to feed in to jealousy, greed, and anger, you are choosing the consequences of those things that are not good. If you choose to pursue joy, peace, love and kindness, you will receive the consequences of those things."

She hated to admit that she liked how the therapist simplified the Cherokee proverb and other questions that she'd asked. Acknowledging that she understood, Aponia sat back in the scoop chair and spun around like a 90-degree top back and forth using her legs to anchor her and build momentum.

"Your parents are paying me to help you. If you are unwilling to help, I can use unspoken cues that you display to gather information about you." Aponia glared back at her resolved to break her down. The therapist returned to her chair and continued to write, occasionally looking at Aponia and back at the clock. The session ended and Aponia was invited to remain in the waiting room while her parents talked to the therapist.

Sharing her thoughts, the therapist summarized the results of the session and assured them that their daughter was strong willed, but capable of being helped once she understood that she would not be giving up on her. Her parents were asked to trust the process and allow her to continue seeing their daughter. The second and third therapy sessions were very similar to the first. Aponia was proving to be strong willed and silent. It had also become a bit of a game for Aponia who was bent on breaking the therapist.

Chapter Six

On their fourth session, the therapist was clad in blue jeans and a white flowered sleeveless shirt. The relaxed fit blue jeans hugged her curvy hips and were accentuated by a black belt at her small waist. Aponia thought she looked like a much younger woman. The therapist invited Aponia to help her in her flower garden outside in the courtyard behind her office. Aponia was suspicious, but agreed to help following her out. Once outside, curiosity got the best of Aponia and she asked questions about the purpose of the flower garden.

"Why do you have a flower garden outside your office?"

The therapist answered, "Well, Aponia Monarch, I wanted to be able to come outside sometime during my work day to be inspired by plants."

"How can flowers inspire you?" Aponia asked kneeling down on the knee board provided to keep from ruining her jeans.

"Just look at them," she smiled spreading her arms wide causing the loose skin on her upper arm to jiggle. "They display their bright colors requiring us to do nothing more than water and fertilize them. They show us their best everyday whether they feel like it or not. This inspires me to be my best whether I feel like it or not."

That made sense Aponia thought. "Why do you want to help me?" she asked looking genuinely curious at her response.

Sitting back on her heals and levering her body up, the therapist crossed to a small bench underneath a tree. "That is a good question, Aponia Monarch. I guess I'd have to say that I genuinely like your parents and I think you deserve to be your best. Lastly, I like helping people…especially those people that challenge me!"

This made Aponia laugh and flutter her eye lashes innocently. "You think I'm a challenge!"

"Yes, but you are also smart, stubborn, and troubled!" the therapist's eye brows arched up daring her to say different. Aponia smiled and pretended to dig in the dirt again.

"Do you think I'm crazy?" Aponia asked looking into the brown eyes that were assessing her.

"No, you're not crazy. You're frustrated because you believe no one really sees you. For some reason, you now question your own sanity about whatever happened to you recently."

How could she know that? She couldn't possibly understand what was in her brain. "What makes you believe that?" Aponia asked warily. "Did my parents tell you about me?"

"No, I didn't need their input, Aponia Monarch!" she smiled at the young confused face. "I have counseled lots of young people and I was one not so long ago."

"You may call me Poni," she smiled feeling silly at having the doctor call her Aponia Monarch repeatedly. She also made a play at bestowing the privilege as a queen would on her vassals. "My parents believe that something is twisted in my brain."

"Thank you. Why do you say that?" the therapist asked returning to pulling weeds around her precious hydrangea with their pink blooms reaching upward toward the sky.

"I went to the building with my boyfriend, Jett." She stopped abruptly and asked, "Do you have to tell my parents everything?"

"No, we can keep some things private if you'd like. However, it would be nice if you did to build rapport and trust with them. They could share your burden if you told them what troubles you eventually."

She continued trusting that Dr. Rochier would keep her word. "We went into the building where we met with Mr. Dex, who gave Jett a key to the apartment on the second floor. We got into an argument and I was hurt. My parents think my mind is twisted, but I know what happened to me." The therapist nodded her agreement. "Jett told my father that he was never there and he moved on days before I was found with his new girlfriend, Jenny."

"What did you and Jett argue about?"

Aponia was quiet for a moment trying to assess whether the therapist believed what she was saying. Determining that she did, the youngster continued, "We decided to run away together months ago. When I showed up at his home unannounced, Jett agreed to run away with me. He called somebody on the phone while he was at his house to let them know a problem had come up. Then, he took me to the building on Gentry Street. We needed money to live on and rent the room." Aponia stopped briefly to form the story in her mind. "We argued because Jett asked me to allow Mr. Dex and his friends to touch me for rent money."

"You refused," the therapist anticipated showing no emotion or judgment.

"Yes, but he said I had no choice," she pleaded for understanding. "He grabbed me and threw me on the bed. In the struggle, I hit my head." Despite his actions, Aponia still held tender feelings for Jett and the doctor didn't miss her subtle cues.

"What did Mr. Dex look like?" she watched Aponia struggle to share her story.

"He was a short, round black man with red eyes. He watched me in a way that made my skin crawl. I knew Jett had done things with Mr. Dex before because he commented about using the same terms as before."

"Did you share this information with your parents?"

"No, when Jett denied being there and Mr. Dex denied seeing me, I kept it to myself. I didn't know if it is real or not."

The therapist touched Aponia's shoulder with her hand and spoke softly, "I believe you. Is it possible that you also didn't want your parents to be mad at Jett." Tears streamed down her face. She couldn't put words to it, but she knew it was true. "You know you can forgive him for yourself without diminishing what he did."

"How can I do that?" she sniffled.

"Forgiveness is the gift that you give yourself," she explained holding her hand. "It helps you to move forward whether the person wronged you ever apologizes. It doesn't mean that you dismiss what they did to you or that you don't hold them accountable. It just releases you to move on."

"I do want to move forward," Aponia cried. "I don't know how to forgive him."

"No worries, we will work on that together." The therapist squeezed Aponia for emphasis.

"Why should you believe me?" she asked trying to gauge her truthfulness.

"Simple. Your explanation answers questions that I've had about the sketchy circumstances that you were found in. I also have been observing you long enough to assess when you're telling the truth. Even if you try to hide it."

Aponia went over to the bench that had been vacated by the doctor. She cried big tears covering her face with her hands. The therapist placed her arms around the youngster trying to comfort her. When the tears subsided, they both sat on the bench in silence enjoying the peace of the garden.

The therapist wanted to distract Aponia from her circumstances by sharing her culture. "In my family, we believe the earth is a living thing." She reached down and picked up a handful of the black, spongy earth and let if fall gently through her fingers. The therapist took off her shoes and put her bare feet on the newly turned earth. She wiggled her toes and raised them so that earth bubbled up at her toes. "Come, share this experience with me."

"No thanks, I don't want to get my feet dirty," Aponia said disbelieving her claim.

"The earth is alive," she smiled. Aponia came closer watching as the doctor's toes peaked out of the earth showing her red nail polish. She sat on the bench and took off her shoes and came to stand next to the doctor. Wiggling her toes, she found it fun and squishy. A smile spread across her golden face.

"How is it alive?" she asked. "It's just dirt and dead stuff."

"It's a lot more than dirt and debris," Dr. Rochier went down to her knees and let the earth crumble and fall through her fingers. "Look closely. Worms, ants, and other insects live here." She dug into the earth further and found a tree root. "Do you know what this is?"

"I think it's some kind of root," Aponia answered honestly peering at the dark brown elongated structure in the soil.

"Correct. This root is attached to the tree over near the bench." Aponia watched in fascination as she pointed to the tree swaying in the breeze waving its rich green foliage at them. She'd known that there were roots under the ground, but never thought much about what they attached to. "That tree gathers nutrients, water, and things it needs to grow through the earth. What you call ordinary dirt is a life line for the trees, insects, animals and people too."

"What's so great about it for people?" Aponia asked looking around and viewing earth in a very different way.

"People plant greens, tomatoes, vegetables, fruit and countless other things in the earth and trust that mother nature will help them grow. The sun, wind, rain, and earth all work together to help plants grow and prosper."

Aponia giggled and wiggled her toes more. Then, she began stomping around in the dirt doing what she called her earth dance. Flapping her arms up and down, back and forth widely as her legs kicked the air and stomped the earth. The therapist enjoyed watching Aponia finally become more animated as a young person. Afterward, Aponia sat down on the bench and found, she'd released energy like she hadn't done in a very long time. She felt better about herself and her situation.

"Why do you think Jett lied about being at the building?" Aponia asked trying to understand how Jett could have betrayed her. She still hated him and didn't know what she'd say when she saw him, but she wanted to know.

"Lots of reasons are possible. It may have been because he was ill equipped to handle a medical emergency where he was not sure whether you would live or die. I suspect he was covering his hind parts by obtaining an alibi in case you were found dead. Most people panic when something horrendous like that happens and he is a youngster himself. It is probably not wise to expect him to react like a seasoned adult."

"I hate him!" Aponia stated simply. "He left me there to die."

The therapist squeezed her arm knowing that Aponia did not hate him nearly as much as she claimed or believed. "Don't judge him too harshly. He is a young man that lied about what he had done. This does not excuse his behavior, but I do not wish for you to be distracted by his betrayal or behavior." Aponia looked confused. "You cannot control his behavior, but you can control your response to it."

"I still hate him!" Aponia repeated vehemently.

"Hate is an emotion that you must pass through and not hold in your soul. Be careful not to be imprisoned by hate to the point that you can no longer move forward with your life."

"How do I move through it," she cried.

"Carefully," the therapist smiled. "It is not easy, but you talk about it, assess it, turn it upside down and view it from different angles. Forgive those who betrayed you, then chart a path to a new future." Aponia didn't believe that she could move forward, but she didn't want to insult Dr. Rochier or her profession. "Some people take longer than others to move through it, but the point is to get to the other side of grief. But I have another question."

Aponia stopped turning the earth with her feet and looked to the doctor. She braced herself for the next question.

"Tell me again why did you run away and what was going on in your life that made running away a viable decision at that moment?"

Aponia thought for a time trying to gauge her own honesty. The therapist told her she could tell if she was not truthful. Resigned, she explained, "A long time ago, Jett said that he wished we could run away together. I didn't think much of the idea at the time."

"Tell me more about what made you think this was a good idea apart from anything that Jett said."

She looked over to her therapist before continuing. "Over the last few weeks, it seemed like the anger and rage inside me was growing out of control. I couldn't get any peace. I was blowing up at everybody over little things. I felt out of control. The night that I ran away I had gotten into an argument with my mother. She called me a drama queen for the umpteenth time. I couldn't take it anymore. So, I ran to Jett's house and convinced him that we should run away. I didn't tell Jett ahead of time because I thought he might say no. I showed up at his house and put him on the spot reminding him that he said we should run away."

The therapist listened intently without judgment. "Jett wasn't really prepared, was he?"

"No, I don't think so," she responded honestly seeing the predicament from a new perspective, Jett's perspective.

"Tell me about the anger and rage."

"Not much to tell. It seems like everything gets on my nerves and makes me angry. I don't know exactly when it started, but it has gotten worse as I've gotten older."

The therapist was looking at her more intently assessing, "Tell me how you feel and what is happening in your body when you feel the rage coming."

Sitting back and closing her eyes, Aponia thought about how it came. "It feels kind of like water on a stove that begins to float little bubbles to the top as it heats. Then the bubbles start to roll up faster and faster until steam is going everywhere."

"What about after the steam leaves?"

Aponia had never tried to isolate the parts of the rage. "I feel like I drop like a rock on the bottom of the pot. I feel sorry about what I've done because I know it wasn't warranted, but it always happens." She looked to the doctor anticipating judgment. She found none.

Aponia went home feeling lightened from the weights that had been plaguing her life. She wasn't responsible for Jett's actions. That had to become her mantra. Repeating it over and over until she could believe it saying, "I am not responsible for anyone else's actions! I am only responsible for my own actions and reactions to others!"

That night, Solomon accused Aponia of going into his room without permission. Aponia felt the old feelings of betrayal and distrust rising from the depths of her soul. "I hate you, Sol! I did not go into your room or touch your things!" She stomped and stomped back and forth in front of his room flailing her arms in the air. His mother tried to calm her daughter. The ranting continued for several minutes until Aponia regained control stomping down the hall and into her bedroom slamming the door behind her.

Solomon stood in the hallway dumb founded. Sophia bounced down the hall singing to herself. She pushed her brother out of the way and entered his room as if she owned it. Sophia picked up her Barbie doll from his shelf shook it in her brother's face causing the doll's long blond hair to tickle her brother's nose.

Solomon had had it with little sisters yelling, "Momma! Momma!" Sophia smiled as if she could not be bothered with his theatrics and danced into the living room. Valerie rolled her eyes and pretended not to hear her eldest. It happened so often she decided to let them figure it out themselves.

Aponia paced her room in front of her bed back and forth as the rage eased and slowed. When she plopped down on the bed, a green and blue stone bounced up in response to her weight on the bed. Something was eerily familiar about the stone. She rubbed the stone enjoying the smooth cold texture. As she rubbed the stone, the remaining negative energy surrounding her ebbed away. Where had she seen the stone before? Where had it come from? She struggled to make the connection. Mr. Billy had a stone similar to this one. Could it be the same one?

Aponia finally gained the courage to share all the details of the night she ran away including her argument with Jett. Valerie and Ethan looked stunned as they quietly listened to their daughter detail the actions leading to her injuries. Valerie found it hard to believe that Jett would expect her daughter to allow men to touch her for money. She wanted to ring his neck with her bare hands. Ethan was seeing red.

"I never liked that lying kid!" he ranted. "To think I actually believed him when he said he was not there the night you were hurt!" Aponia watched embarrassed and unsure of how to proceed. "I'm going to the police and have him arrested along with that man, Mr. Dex!" Ethan rubbed his head trying to process the information that he had been given by his daughter.

Later that evening, Officer Bert Gleeson came to the house for a follow up report. Ethan related the story that had been given to him by Aponia. Officer Gleeson sat at the kitchen table with a clip board and pen recording information on a preprinted form. He had recorded the case number, victim information, contact information and related information from previous reports. Officer Gleeson's brown eyes watched intently as Aponia went through her story start to finish without interrupting. He carefully wrote questions down one side of a piece of lined paper organizing his thoughts.

After Aponia completed her thoughts and released a deep breath, Officer Gleeson asked the questions that he had written down the side of the page. After he felt like he had a complete picture with all pertinent details, we sat back in the seat and looked from Valerie, Ethan and Aponia.

"Thank you for being so forthright with your details," he smiled at Aponia. "I know that this has not been easy."

"Are you going to arrest him?" Ethan asked fury still in his voice. "He could have killed my daughter!"

"We will conduct a thorough investigation," Officer Gleeson stated holding Ethan's attention. "We have to be able to prove the allegations."

"It's obvious that he was there," Ethan complained. "How would Poni know what Mr. Dex looked like and where he stayed? They lied!"

"I will be asking those questions and writing my reports. After that, I will make a referral to the District Attorney if it is warranted." Officer Gleeson spoke as a matter of fact. "I don't want to promise you more than what I can deliver. I will do my best!" He rose from the table and said good bye to the family. Ethan wasn't convinced that Officer Gleeson could get a conviction by his noncommittal attitude. He wanted to pound on Jett until sense poured into his brain.

Aponia felt relieved to have everything out in the open. Hate was such a strong word for what she was feeling toward Jett, but she would find a better word in time. The betrayal and leaving her for dead had bothered her most. According to her therapist, she couldn't get caught up in the cycle of hate. Her parents made it easy for her to feel justified in wanting bad things to happen to Jett for his part in her injuries. For now, it was all too overwhelming to process.

Chapter Seven

During her next therapy session, Aponia found she needed to share something that deeply troubled her. Memories had returned from her time in the hospital. She needed to understand Mr. Billy and why his memories had troubled her so. This was a big step. She had not dared talk about Mr. Billy after leaving the hospital because she was sure that her therapist would deem her certifiably crazy. None of it made any sense to her.

Aponia asked that they work in the garden while they talked. The therapist wore her blue jean pants torn just above one knee and a thin t-shirt to accommodate the 95-degree heat. Knowing what made a patient comfortable to share their vulnerabilities was critical for creating a comfortable sharing environment.

Aponia began as soon as they found their knee pads and began tugging at weeds and turning the earth. "This may sound crazy, but I had strange memory from the hospital." Aponia shared all the information uninterrupted as her therapist listened. No one in the family recognized the man named William Green or Mr. Billy.

"He knew very personal things about me that no one but my family would know. For example, I was born with an um…um…umbilical cord around my neck and that I have butterfly wings on my left shoulder blade." The therapist continued to listen finding the story intriguing. "I didn't know about the um…um…biblical cord around my neck was until he said it and my mom confirmed it. And, he knew that my nickname with my family is Poni."

The therapist summarized the information provided, "Mr. Billy fought in the Battle of Honey Springs on July 17, 1863. So, we can assume that he lived more than 160 years ago." She repeated the facts creating a time line in her mind. "He showed you a blue and green calming stone at one point." Aponia nodded her head in agreement.

Aponia breathed deeply and held out the blue green stone in her hand that she'd found on her bed. The therapist pulled the stone from her palm and carefully turned the stone this way and that. Its color was a deep rich blue green. Its surface was smooth and cold as if held in a cold place for a long period. It contained positive energy that she could feel.

"Mr. Billy showed you this stone?" she asked trying to wrap her mind around the story that she was being told. She held up the stone in the light to ensure that it was real.

"I almost thought that Mr. Billy was a figment of my imagination until the stone showed up. He told me that he couldn't rest until what was stolen by war was returned to his family."

The therapist had never heard a story like this one. She didn't know what to make of it. Something compelled her to believe Aponia and help her with the answers she needed.

"When he needed to calm down, he stroked the stone next to a creek. That was his place of peace."

"Have you chosen a place of peace?" the doctor asked curiously. She wanted to take Aponia's assertions seriously. She needed to be heard and felt down deep that she was destined to be part of the solution for her young charge.

Aponia shook her head no in response. "I didn't know that I needed to."

"I think it is time. Take the stone and keep it in your pocket or purse. When you feel anxious, rub the stone to find your place of peace."

"How do I choose a place of peace?" Aponia wanted to know.

The therapist sat next to her patient. "You have to look around and try to find a place where you feel comfortable, safe and quiet. This will allow you to take time to think and gain control of your emotions. You will know when you've found it. The stone will help as well. When you feel the anger beginning to bubble, it's time to focus on rubbing the stone and physically transporting your body to that special place."

It was Aponia's mission to find her calming place. With the calming stone in her pocket, she moved around to each room inside the house and sat quietly waiting for a sign or feeling or something to tell her this was her place. Nothing. She walked outside in the front yard and immediately ruled out all the spaces because they were too noisy for her to relax.

With Rowdy at her heels, she walked around the small backyard with her bare feet on the earth. The therapist had taught her that energy could be transferred through your bare feet. She walked out to the swing set near the back wooden fence. Dusting off the slightly rusted seat, she sat. She and her siblings had enjoyed the swing and jungle gym as younger children. Swinging leisurely, she waited for something to reveal itself. Nothing.

She went inside the small gazebo at the center of the yard with its white vinyl structure covered in honey suckle. The air was filled with the smell of honey suckle flowers blooming all around. The flowers were so dense that it was difficult to know if anyone was sitting inside.

Aponia sat down and put Rowdy onto her lap. Something was different here. She sat quietly and remarkably so did Rowdy. The breeze blew ruffling the sides of her curly hair. Relaxing her shoulders, Aponia's mind drifted and cleared. Breathing deeply taking in the honey suckle, she could taste its pungent scent on her tongue. Rowdy lay down on her nap. This was it. This was her place of peace. She pulled the calming stone from her pocket and rubbed it experimentally. It felt wonderful in her fingers, cold and calming. Aponia closed her eyes to enjoy the solitude.

Although she could not wrap her mind around everything, she did trust that her therapist had her best interest. She would wait and see if the process worked. Aponia was committed to seeing the process through whether good or bad.

Acknowledging that there was line between professional and personal help, the therapist discussed the delineation between the two and proposed a plan moving forward with Valerie and Ethan. Professionally, the therapist wanted to maintain perspective in helping Aponia so that she received her very best therapy. However, there were multiple layers that needed to be explored and part of it layered into her personal life passion, genealogy. They had to be clear where lines were drawn and understand how and why she would make the suggestions that she did. It wasn't about the money, but establishing clear boundaries.

At the therapist's urging, Aponia shared the story of Mr. Billy and all the details including the calming stone with her parents. They found many parts of the story unbelievable but vowed to support their daughter. The next therapy session was conducted jointly to allow all concerned and their varying perspectives. Each were encouraged to be honest about what they believed and did not believe.

Because the story of Mr. Billy was fantastical, the therapist wanted all cards on the table so that they could work through any issues that related to their plan moving forward. All understood that there was a rage or anger that had been passed down through Mr. Billy's family that apparently had some connection to the Monarch family. However, because Mr. Billy sought Aponia out, there had to be a reason for sharing it with her in particular. The therapist suspected a pattern of behavior with anger and rage, but could not be sure at the moment.

Reviewing the entire runaway story, they broke the events down into distinguishable parts. First, Aponia has been plagued with a rage or anger that had been getting progressively worse with age. This was no one's fault and no one should feel any guilt related to it. "It is simply what it was," she explained. Second, Aponia chose to runaway to escape the rage and anger that she was experiencing. She thought Jett offered her love and stability that she needed to escape the pain.

"Her boyfriend, Jett, did not entice her to runaway although he may have agreed to go with her." The therapist made it clear that Jett had responsibility for injuring Aponia and leaving to cover his own hind parts. Ethan's jaws were tight in response to Jett's part in his daughter's plight. "Don't be distracted by the periphery issues and maintain the focal point, Aponia, her health and well-being."

Ethan voiced his feelings of anger toward Jett and Mr. Dex, but agreed to remain focused on his daughter and her needs. To Ethan's credit, he acknowledged that he understood no one was absolving anyone from their responsibility. Their purpose was to support Aponia and her needs. Jett and Mr. Dex continued to deny either being with Aponia or meeting her on the night she was injured. There was no proof to the contrary. Ethan had even believed Jett when he said he moved on and never went to the building with her.

As for her therapist, she believed that Jett had taken Aponia to the building without the where-with-all to handle the medical emergency. He panicked and ran home when he thought Aponia had been accidentally hurt. Remembering that good or bad, he is a fifteen-year-old kid that didn't know what to do. This was not an excuse but an attempt to see things from a different perspective.

"In any case, Aponia decided to run away to escape the pain in her life related to the anger and rage that seems to be plaguing her. This is the real problem she explained." The therapist summarized her thoughts and offered the bottom line. "Aponia needs help managing this rage and for some unknown reason Mr. Billy has reached out to her." Valerie and Ethan were both stunned that the therapist believed the Mr. Billy story. They had not believed their daughter's recounting of the encounter initially.

"You believe the story of Mr. Billy?" Ethan asked looking into her brown eyes.

She took off her glasses and looked into Ethan's hazel eyes. She paused for emphasis before answering, "Yes, I do. Her recounting of the story of Mr. Billy is very detailed and confirmed with the blue green calming stone."

"What is a calming stone?" Valerie asked unbelieving. "How do we know she didn't just find the stone and added it to the story?"

"After getting to know your daughter, I have come to know her very well. She is very clear about Mr. Billy and I believe he is real to her. This is not typical. I believe Mr. Billy has a mission to save your daughter. He apparently suffered from a similar affliction."

Ethan and Valerie still didn't believe or understand the situation with Mr. Billy, but were willing to trust the therapeutic process. She wanted to explore who Mr. Billy was and find out why and how he wanted to help Aponia. This would be more of a personal relationship because it did not have a professional foundation for therapeutic treatment at this time. They would need to explore the Monarch genealogy and history. Aponia's parents agreed to allow the new plan to move forward. A blending of professional and personal plan would help their daughter solve the mystery of Mr. Billy and his relationship to the rage plaguing her.

Excited that she was believed, Aponia was willing to investigate her family's history and verify Mr. Billy's claims. The rage had become disruptive to her life and she could no longer excuse it or ignore it. Aponia's first task was to interview her relatives and create a family tree.

Her therapist, who had embarked on a similar genealogy journey as a teenager, provided blank genealogy forms and interview sheets with prompts for names, addresses, contact information, relationships, and stories about the previous generations. Aponia became a genealogical scientist for her family and her therapist served as her assistant.

Aponia started with her parents asking questions about their parents, stories that they had heard and where ancestors had been buried. After writing information on her forms, she outlined what questions were left unanswered. Aponia was so excited about learning about her family. In the past, she had not understood the importance of her family's history. She collected as much information and together they'd analyze it.

During the next therapy session, the therapist wore slim jeans that proved more slimming to her hips, a green short sleeve sweater and her red converse tennis shoes. Aponia admired her ability to look professional and comfortable all at once. She seemed more like her big sister than a therapist. They scattered all the family tree forms and other papers across the table in her office.

Organizing the papers, they sat to transcribe the family information shared by Mr. Billy. Aponia lounged in the brown scoop chair adjacent to the doctor's desk and repeated all the information that she remembered. While Aponia closed her eyes trying to recall what Mr. Billy shared, the therapist took notes carefully filling in a family tree and making notes. They needed to see if there was an overlap in the two families. Otherwise, they would continue to investigate until they found what connected Mr. Billy to Aponia, if anything.

With the details captured on paper, she read the information back to Aponia, "William Green or Mr. Billy had a son named William Green who they called Little Billy. There may be other children, but Little Billy, like his father exhibited an anger or rage." Aponia nodded her agreement. "Little Billy married a woman named Harriet and they had a son named Arthur. Again, there may be other children, but Mr. Billy was very specific in focusing on this line of children. Arthur married Betsy and had a son named Fred. Both Arthur and Fred exhibited the rage and we are assuming that Mr. Billy tried to contact them as well."

"I assumed that, but he didn't tell me that he exactly contacted them both because he was trying to help his children and grandchildren."

The therapist agreed with her assessment. Aponia smiled feeling mature and grown up at her analysis of Mr. Billy's story. "Fred Green married Clara and they had a son name Alex Green."

"If none of his children were in the war, how could they have gotten the anger or rage like their father?" Aponia asked looking at the pages and tree for connectors.

"There is something called epigenetics," her therapist explained. "Epeee-genetics," she sounded the word out for Aponia. "It means that a trauma that was experienced by Mr. Billy could possibly be passed on to future generations. Native Americans talked about this hundreds of years ago. Other cultures only recently started to study what they've known for a long time."

"Epeee-Genetics," Aponia sounded the word out. "Funny name for passing things down to your children." Her therapist laughed at Aponia's ability to simplify her statement.

"If I understand correctly, Mr. Billy is unable to rest because the trauma that started with him is still being passed down to his children and grandchildren. He is unable to have peace because he can't stop it." Aponia thought about the summation and nodded her head in agreement. "Keep going with your story."

"Let me see, Alex Green married a lady named Dorian and they had a daughter named Kittie Green. I don't remember anything after that."

The therapist continued filling in pages and writing notes. Afterward, the two spread the new pages on the table reviewing the pages for overlaps. Nothing seemed to overlap. The doctor decided to gather newspaper articles, obituaries, cemetery headstones and any other information she could find related the people that they had identified thus far. Aponia's job was to continue to interview relatives and go back as far as she could with her family members.

Dr. Rochier scheduled a field trip to the Battle of Honey Springs Visitor's Center with Aponia to learn more about what Mr. Billy may have experienced and gain perspective from the story that he shared. On the first Saturday of April, she drove Aponia to the Honey Springs Battle Field in her Silver Porsche Macan. Once inside, Aponia ran her hand over the leather seats and smooth console between the seats.

The dash board was covered with flashing buttons, lights and gadgets reminding Aponia of an airplane cockpit that she'd seen in video games. The therapist looked over her white heart shaped sunglasses admiring the way the youngster cooed over the interior of the vehicle. Aponia was clad in blue jeans, a light weight summer top and red converse. Her therapist wore blue jeans, a short sleeve cotton top with flowers, and brown comfortable walking shoes. After placing the seat belt diagonally across her body and clicking it into place, they were on their way to a short drive to the battle field.

A short time later, the pair arrived at the 1863 Honey Springs Battle Field Visitor's Center. The parking lot was paved with signs directing visitors to the front of the tan and brown metal structure with columns that served as the Visitor's Center. The two rustic columns held up the wooden portico just outside the double glass front doors and a second story above. Flanking both sides of the front door were two chocolate colored building wings. With only about a hand full of cars in the parking lot, the pair entered through the front door, asked for information and paid the entrance fee. The receptionist, a ruddy faced teenage boy who looked to be about sixteen, collected the money, provided brochures, and directed them to the east side of the building to see the exhibits.

The two started with a short video reenactment of the Battle of Honey Springs. They marveled at the tasteful way the video documented the battle, death, and honored the soldiers who fought and gave their lives. She was unsure how Aponia would react to the violence depicted in the documentary. Pleasantly surprised, Aponia didn't seem overly concerned about what she was seeing.

Next, they moved to the east end of the center where fourteen audio players provided recordings of first hand, and written accounts from the soldiers who fought at the Battle of Honey Springs. The museum also had exhibits displaying firearms, ammunition and artillery used in the battle. Aponia moved around the room reading the information. Nothing had captured her attention yet and her therapist was careful to watch for unusual reactions or outward signs of distress such as crying, rapid breathing or avoiding certain displays. The youngster displayed no abnormal signs of distress.

Leaving the visitor center, they retrieved back packs filled with light refreshments including water, chips, and a chicken sandwich from the trunk of the car. Then they were off to explore a portion of the 1,000-acre historical site. The site consisted of rolling hills covered in green grass that crunched underneath their feet and wild flowers of purple, white, yellow and blue. The site was dotted here and there with other visitors who nodded and smiled as they passed them.

Dr. Rochier read literature from the brochure out loud provided in the museum and summarized for Aponia. In 1863, the United States government relocated peace keeping troops from what had been Indian Territory. Many Native Americans had been forced to the area as a result of the Trail of Tears, a forced relocation of Native American from the East coast to Indian Territory. Soon after the government withdrew their troops, the Confederate States signed treaties of alliance with the Five Tribes, and for a year or so no one challenged Confederate control of Indian Territory.

Then, Federal authority challenged the Confederacy to reestablish its authority in Indian Territory. The Confederate installation at Honey Springs consisted of a frame commissary building, a log hospital, several arbors, and a multitude of tents. The springs provided water for soldiers and the livestock.

She explained, "This was an important area because the Texas Road was the main transportation route connecting Indian Territory, Texas, Kansas and Missouri. So, this was a valuable place because of the water resources and established road for stage coaches and other forms of transportation running through the territory."

"Why didn't they just negotiate and buy the rights to the property from the people here?" Aponia asked. "Seems like a lot of fighting that could have been avoided."

The therapist smiled and commented, "You're not wrong, but sometimes people don't do the obvious. Both sides thought they were right and were willing to fight over it."

Aponia shook her head in disgust, "Men, they never learn." The doctor laughed at her comment before beginning the trek up a trail.

The two made their way over hills to an area marked with signage indicating that the First Kansas Colored Volunteer Regiment had fought on the front line in the area. She motioned for Aponia to stop. Aponia read the sign and realized that Mr. Billy had spoken about the First Kansas Regiment. They stopped in the shade of a small tree to enjoy the moment in the cool canopy below the tree. Together, they shared a small blanket for refreshments. They ate while Dr. Rochier read information about what happened on that faithful day.

The battle lasted four hours and ended by 2:00 p.m. Colonel James M. Williams was the commanding officer of the First Kansas Colored Volunteer Infantry Regiment and the regiment was near the center of the Federal line. The Confederate and Federal lines fired back and forth simultaneously. At the height of the battle, the Federal Second Indian Home Guard Regiment unintentionally moved between the First Kansas Regiment and the Texas dismounted calvary regiments. Colonel Williams had been injured and his successor was Lieutenant Colonel John Bowles, who ordered the Federal Second Indian Home Guard Regiment to fall back.

Misunderstanding the command, the Confederate dismounted calvary units heard the order to fall back and moved forward in pursuit. The Confederates approached to within 25 paces of the Federals and were met with a volley from the deadly accurate Springfield rifles of the Kansas Colored Regiment. Aponia understood the gravity of what she was hearing. This lined up with what Mr. Billy had told her.

"Mr. Billy fought with the First Kansas Colored Regiment," Aponia gulped hard with her eyes bugged out. She looked around her seeing more than what she had before. "This is where he and the other soldiers fought." She touched the ground reverently removing her shoes to feel the ground with her bare feet. The therapist did the same watching Aponia carefully to ensure that she did not injure her feet on the stubbly grass or sharp objects that may hidden in the grass or earth.

"Because of a mistake, they were able to turn the battle in their direction within seconds," she breathed deeply. "He served with great courage and deserves great honor."

"How many soldiers were killed?"

The therapist looked through the literature trying to find the answer. "The Confederate leaders reported losses of 134 killed and wounded with 47 taken prisoner. Union leaders reported their losses as seventeen killed and sixty wounded. No one knows for sure."

Aponia said a little prayer for the men who lost their lives fighting for what they believed. She continued reading the brochure further indicating that the unmarked graves may still be in the Honey Springs area. The bodies of the Federal dead were later interred in the Fort Gibson National Cemetery.

Aponia walked a short distance to a historical marker that read, "General Blunt heaped praise on the Black men who fought with him at Honey Springs. He said of them in his official report on the battle: "The First Kansas (colored) particularly distinguished itself; they fought like veterans, and preserved their line unbroken throughout the engagement. Their coolness and bravery have never been surpassed; they were in the hottest of the fight, and opposed to Texas troops twice their number, whom they completely routed. One Texas regiment (the Twentieth Calvary) that fought against them went into the fight with 300 men and came out with only sixty." Tears trickled down their cheeks. Mr. Billy had been right. He and the other soldiers served with honor in this place.

"He was telling the truth about his service," Aponia cried. She touched the sign and prayed for peace feeling honored that she was able to hear his story.

Her therapist put her hand on Aponia's shoulder and said softly, "This is only part of his story. When he came home, he brought with him the trauma of this fight." Aponia turned in comfort and cried in earnest for Mr. Billy and what he endured.

"Do you think Mr. Billy could be buried in the Fort Gibson National Cemetery?" Aponia asked looking for ways to connect to Mr. Billy.

She thought for a minute. "It's a possibility." After some thought, she proposed that they take a trip out to the cemetery and see if he is buried there. Aponia was excited at the possibility of finding out more about Mr. Billy.

After continuing their trek across the vast battle field, they learned more about the diversity of men that fought and died on both sides.

Aponia stopped to listen periodically to see if she could hear any voices from the past. She heard none, but hoped all found peace.

An hour later, Aponia was dropped off at her home. She waved as she slid out of the cockpit of the vehicle and closed the door behind her. Aponia shared what she had learned with her family. She was excited to know that Mr. Billy's story was confirmed by the history found at the Honey Springs Battlefield and Visitor Center.

Chapter Eight

On the following Saturday, the therapist picked up Aponia in front of her small ranch style home. Aponia waved good bye to her mother and Solomon as she ran toward the Silver Porsche. The Fort Gibson National Cemetery was a half hour from Aponia's home. Creating a strategy, the pair agreed on a plan of investigation for eliminating and proving information. The small concrete office with both a giant U.S. flag and the State of Oklahoma flags floated atop the flag poles outside the office.

She pulled the silver Porsche in front of the office on the half-moon shaped drive way. A starched and pressed young man in a green camouflage uniform stood as they entered the office. He was tall and slim with his matching shirt neatly tucked into his pants. His camouflage hat too sat squarely on his head as his olive skin, brown eyes and serious demeanor did not betray his inner thoughts.

Dr. Rochier smiled brightly and introduced herself to the young man. He shook her hand and inquired about how he could help. After explaining who they were looking for, he accessed his computer database for the cemetery. Within minutes, he located three men named William Green. Since they had limited information in which to distinguish one from another. The soldier provided a map of the cemetery and circled the location of each headstone. From that, they hoped to gather dates of birth and/or death and any other information that may be present on the headstone. Because Mr. Billy served during the Civil War, he would have been a young man of at least 20 in 1863. That would serve as a clue to eliminate one or more of the men.

The Fort Gibson National Cemetery headstones stood in neatly lined sections that were separated by concrete walkways and United States flags. Although there were thousands of neatly and precisely positioned headstones, the pair followed the map provided by the soldier. The first headstone was found in section G, row seven. Aponia jumped up and down excitedly when she located the headstone that said William Green. The pair knelt down before the headstone to better see the information. Aponia touched it reverently as she read the date of birth and death. William Green was born on September 11, 1901 and died on April 4, 2000.

"Do you think that it is our Mr. Billy?" Aponia asked quietly. This place demanded respect and reverence to her mind with the gently blowing flags, neatly groomed landscape and hallowed feel.

"Poni, I don't think so. He was born after 1863 when we know that he served at the Battle of Honey Springs. I'm sorry, but this is not him." She patted Aponia's hand lightly. Disappointment showed on Aponia's face as tears trickled down her face.

The pair waved good bye to the headstone and went in search of the second headstone. It was located in the back of the cemetery where older graves were marked. The headstones in section CC were neatly lined up and kept, but some were white headstones that stood above ground and others lay flat to the ground where mowers could easily cut over them. They walked down the aisle to row three and counted four markers over. The grave marker lay flat to the earth in white marble with the name William Green written on its face. The person was born in 1850 and died in 1901.

Aponia heart began to feel excited. This William Green was born before 1863. She was afraid to believe it might be him. She went to her knees and ran her small fingers across the face of the headstone. "Are you Mr. Billy?" she asked quietly. The therapist sat down next to Aponia and touched her arm. "What do you think?"

Looking at the birth and death date, the therapist calculated the man's age when the Battle of Honey Creek occurred. "He would have been thirteen years old when the battle took place. Since he had escaped from Arkansas with his wife and children before coming to Indian Territory, it is unlikely that he would be old enough for our Mr. Billy." Aponia looked disappointed, but understood the logic.

Again, they waved to the headstone and looked for the last William Green. They found him not far away on row one. The white headstone stood up from the ground aligned with several others on the row. Aponia looked to her therapist as she read the name and the years of birth and death and the inscription "Rest in Peace, husband and father".

"He was born in 1829 and died in 1931 which made him 102."

"He would have been 34 during the battle. It is possible that he could have had a wife and children at this time," the therapist calculated the dates in her head and speculated about possibilities. "This bears more investigation." Aponia grinned widely and ran her hand across the headstone. The therapist took a photo of the headstone with her cell phone and noted the location on the back of the map provided by the soldier. They were both hopeful that they'd found Mr. Billy's final resting place and that he would one day rest in peace.

"Are you Mr. Billy?" she repeated as they said their final farewells. "Until we meet again." She felt nothing in response.

The therapist and her protege sifted through records to find William Green born in 1829 and served in the military. Genealogy programs, newspapers, on-line databases were scoured in an effort to find Mr. Billy. Looking over the top of her glasses like her mentor when she was in deep thought, Aponia had taken to pushing her glasses onto the end of her nose. When the therapist glanced up to find Aponia mimicking her actions, they both burst into laughter. They enjoyed being with one another. Gone were the days of awkwardness and embarrassment. Aponia felt that she could talk to her about her fears and vulnerabilities.

The days turned into weeks and the search continued. The articles regarding military stories of heroism did not include this William Green or he couldn't be ruled out as Mr. Billy. They needed more clues. The therapist asked Aponia to sit and think about any other information that she could remember about Mr. Billy. She sat in the scoop chair slumped with the toes of her shoes anchored to the floor as she moved the chair slowly back and forth.

"I think his wife was named Hattie," Aponia finally said. "Can we search for her?"

The therapist had an idea. She searched for articles, marriage records and any other information for Hattie and William Green with the children he'd mentioned. The search narrowed to two men one born in 1875 and the other born in 1825. None were born in 1829. However, some records were copied in error and a difference of four years was not impossible to make. Therefore, they could not rule out the William Green found in the cemetery. The search continued.

Taking a slightly different approach, she instructed Aponia to go to the oldest person in her family and see if anyone was familiar with the last name given by Mr. Billy. Over the next two weeks, Aponia contacted her Uncle Rory for assistance with their family history. He had been a child, but paid close attention to family gossip, funerals, celebrations and other events. When there were family questions, he was the one contacted.

One weekend, Ethan and Valerie drove their children to visit Uncle Rory. All watched as the broad-shouldered man with the big personality carted out a trunk filled with pictures and memorabilia. Uncle Rory stroked his mustache and beard with his big hands as he opened the trunk and contemplated where to begin. Valerie held Sophia tightly in her lap so that she did not interfere with Aponia's search. Sophia liked attention and sometimes asked questions to gain the spotlight. Because of their limited time with Uncle Rory, she wanted keep Sophia corralled in her lap. Ethan watched trying to absorb as much information as he could.

One by one, he pulled out batches of pictures sharing what information that he knew about them. Aponia shared the information that Mr. Billy had shared with her and all the names of the generations of children that she could remember. After about an hour, Uncle Rory pulled out a yellowed obituary of a beautiful woman named Alice Green Monarch. Some information on the paper had faded and was almost unreadable. However, the first line read Alice Green Monarch was the daughter of Kittie Green and Daniel Monarch. Time stopped for Aponia.

When she was able to regain her speech, Aponia explained, "Kittie Green was one of the names mentioned by Mr. Billy." Uncle Rory read what he could of the background and history of Alice Green Monarch. The woman in the black and white photo had straight hair that ended just past her shoulders appearing to be in her early twenties. She was wearing a button-down dress sitting on a small stool. The background had faded eliminating clues for a time period when the picture was taken. "Could this be their connection?" Aponia whispered more to herself than to the audience surrounding her. They read the information several times gleaning that Alice died in 1993 and had been buried in the Honey Springs Cemetery in the family plot.

Uncle Rory placed the obituary on the table while they continued their search of the trunk. Nothing else offered any clues to the Green family were found. When they had finished, Valerie took a photo of the front and back of the obituary with her cell phone and Uncle Rory placed the original obituary in a plastic sleeve for safe keeping. An hour later, they were on their way home and Aponia was about to jump out of her skin with excitement.

While Aponia had been investigating her family, her therapist had been working to verify or rule out the remaining William Greens that they'd found. She was able to verify that the William Green born in 1829 had a wife named Elizabeth and no children. There were no mentions of multiple marriages, so he was eliminated based on the information available.

The William Green born in 1875 was eliminated based on his birth after the Battle of Honey Springs. The remaining William Green born in 1825 was listed as an Irish immigrant in his military records that migrated to the United States in 1900. Since he was not in the United States during the Battle of Honey Springs, he too was eliminated from their list of possibles for Mr. Billy.

During their next therapy session, they shared progress on the Mr. Billy saga. The therapist outlined her logic for eliminating the three William Greens. Aponia shared her exciting news and Valerie provided a copy of the obituary information. She looked at the obituary reviewing each line carefully. The information available was consistent with what Mr. Billy provided. Aponia wondered why her therapist was not about to come unglued like she was. Excitement simply oozed out of her pores.

"Is she the one?" Aponia asked excitedly.

The therapist continued to read as Aponia and Valerie looked on. "I am very encouraged," she smiled.

"What?" Aponia asked excitedly. "Why aren't you excited?"

She laughed and explained, "I am excited, but in genealogy we must be driven by facts. I don't want you to get excited and stop looking to verify information further." Aponia deflated like a balloon losing its air.

"Ok, how do we do that?" she asked. She went behind her desk to review more notes and plot a new plan to verify new clues working backward from Kittie Green Monarch.

She explained that they needed to get as much information about Kittie's parents and grandparents, which may be in the cemetery. If they can do that, they can go to on-line databases and start working backward to see if the information aligns with Mr. Billy's family history. She reminded Aponia that Mr. Billy may have been their relatives' best friend or neighbor. It was clear that Mr. Billy knew her family well, but that didn't mean they were directly related. There was more work to do. Resigned, Aponia agreed to go to the cemetery with Uncle Rory to see if they can find more family.

Before concluding their session, the therapist wanted to discuss how Aponia was dealing with the anger and rage. Things had calmed some because she'd been distracted with Mr. Billy's research. However, there had been two outbursts at school. One occurred when a classmate teased her about Jenny taking her boyfriend. This resulted in Aponia being sent to the Dean's office and her parents called. After two days in detention, the matter was resolved.

The second outburst came when she saw Jett and Jenny holding hands walking home from school. She'd seen red and called Jett a name that her mother and father would not approve. He and Jenny, his perfect Jenny with dark curly hair and long thin legs, flicked her off like she was not there and walked away. Aponia was embarrassed that she had been unable to control herself in the moment and then to be ignored was beyond disrespect.

After taking several refreshing breaths, Aponia began, "I know that I didn't control myself. He didn't come after me although I wanted to hurt him like he hurt me."

"How did you feel afterward?" she looked over the top of her glasses as Aponia often mimicked her. "Did the outburst help you feel better?"

"I didn't feel better. I felt embarrassed in front of my classmates because I started it. And no, I didn't feel better," Aponia said sarcastically anticipating the next question. "I should have thought through my actions when I first felt the flicker of anger. I knew it was coming and I did nothing to stop it."

"What do you think you should do next time?"

"I'll stop, acknowledge that its happening and then take deep breaths," Aponia began. "Then I can rub my stone, walk away and/or go to my calming place. I ran head long into it because I was angry with him."

After a time, Aponia relaxed back in the scoop chair watching her mother's reactions. She thought she'd see anger at her lack of control, but was pleasantly surprised that she saw neither. She had hoped to dodge the conversation about her outbursts, but felt better afterward.

Once she returned home, Aponia started her chores. Taking out the white plastic garbage bag to the 80-gallon green trash bin was her chore. She lifted the plastic black lid and threw the bag inside. Over her shoulder, she noticed a stocky young man with rich brown eyes and braces standing just over six foot tall. He was a little older than Aponia but she recognized her childhood friend, Loki Kincaid, immediately. They had been inseparable in elementary school until Aponia had an outburst with him. Afterward, he had simply walked away without retaliating. Aponia supposed he had been waiting for an apology, but she never had the courage to do it.

"What's up squirt!" he smiled approaching from his two- story neighboring home. Their properties shared an alleyway between the properties and a chain link fence that separated the two. The Kincaid home was a two-story contemporary with long black lines that outlined windows across the back of the house and several plate glass windows in the front. The black lines were complimented by bold coffee colored siding that fit perfectly with the rustic feel of the neighborhood. He put his hands in his pockets as he stood next to her. Aponia could hardly believe he was talking to her at all.

"Hi, Lo," she answered warily. "What's up?"

"Nothing, just came over to say hello."

Aponia had been heading to the gazebo for quiet time and wasn't really in the mood for company. "Not a good time. Heading to the gazebo for some quiet time," she gave him a hint to leave as she started toward the backyard.

"Noticed that you spend time in there lately," Loki smiled knowingly.

She stopped in her tracks and turned toward him suspiciously. "How do you know that?"

"My window is right up there," he pointed. "Remember."

"You're spying on me?" she stopped putting her hands on her hips and confronting him.

"No. Just noticed when I was in my room. You've been there, you know it looks down on your backyard."

Silly, Aponia did know that. They had spent time as kids pitching water balloons on Solomon from there. "I remember. Thanks for stopping by." She resumed her trek to the gazebo hoping that he would not continue following her and take the hint to leave. He didn't. He followed her to the rounded structure of the gazebo where the smell of honey suckles permeated the air all around them. Aponia cleared the wooden seating area that followed the rounded perimeter of the gazebo of dust and leaves before sitting down. Loki didn't wait to be asked to sit across from her with his long legs crossed at the ankles.

"What do you want?" Aponia asked giving him the evil eye.

"Nothing," he answered crossing his arms across his chest. "I heard that we were seeing the same therapist." Aponia was stunned for a moment.

"How do you know that?"

"I overheard your mother talking to mine," he explained. "My mother is the one who gave your mother the information about the therapist." Aponia's anxiety eased a bit and she relaxed her back against the lattice work of the gazebo.

"Are you crazy?" Aponia asked unfairly.

"No, are you?" Loki hit back.

"No," she admitted. "Sorry, that was unfair." Loki nodded his head acknowledging her apology.

"We used to have fun together. And…I might be able to help."

She eyed him sitting more erect again. "With what?"

He laughed. "Your situation." Aponia wasn't sure what he knew and what he didn't so she watched waiting for more information. "Several things actually. You had anger issues long before you and Jett hooked up. And then, there is the Jenny thing."

Angrily she asked, "What Jenny thing?"

Loki explained that he'd been seeing the therapist for several years after the death of his grandmother. He was having trouble coping with the grief. Before that, he'd had a confrontation with Aponia. She had called him names and said he was a fat blob that no one would ever like. Loki was devastated hearing the words from his best friend. Looking back, he recognized the outbursts of Aponia with many of his friends. They'd gotten progressively worse until she bit him too. Because she'd never apologized, he'd severed the friendship and vowed to never talk to her again.

Then, his mother asked that he assist his old friend with her struggles especially after she was injured. He didn't immediately agree, but later acquiesced. From what he had learned, Jett abandoned

Aponia after injuring her. Jenny on the other hand had offered another perspective altogether. Loki wasn't sure how Aponia would take the news, but he thought she needed to know.

Guilt had been plaguing Aponia for her unfair treatment of her friend. She looked at her friend and apologized saying, "Lo, I was wrong to say those hurtful things to you. This is long overdue. I apologize from the bottom on my heart."

He smiled and accepted her apology. Aponia smiled back at her friend that she had missed for years. She shared what happened the night that she had run away with Jett. Trying to be fair about everything, she included her part in asking Jett to run away with her without any notice of what she planned. The therapist had encouraged her to be honest with friends and family and accept responsibility for her actions. Loki would recognize and understand this as well.

"Jett told his friends that you were lying to get back at him for dumping you and dating Jenny," Loki began again. "He said that you made up all that stuff about him wanting you to let people touch you."

"Do you believe him," Aponia asked genuinely.

"Not anymore," Loki punched his friend lightly on the shoulder. "I know how hard this is for you to tell me about what happened. I am sorry that he would even ask that you allow men to touch you." Tears leaked from her eyes. This was the first time she'd shared that information with a friend. Aponia breathed deeply and leaned back against the lattice work structure. She took the calming stone from her pocket and rubbed it liberally. Loki watched fascinated.

After some time, she asked, "What about Jenny?"

"She is a piece of work. I call her a collector because she collects men like trophies. Don't get me wrong she is pretty and all, but she doesn't really feel much for Jett." Aponia looked confused. Loki continued, "Jenny is dating Jett and three other men."

"What?" Aponia asked not absorbing what she was hearing.

"Jett told the police and everybody else that he and Jenny had been dating. They were except Jett was not the only one dating her. Jett thinks himself in love with Jenny, but she told a couple of her friends that she only wants him for what he can give her. And she doesn't like the negative attention attached to you, so she is going to dump him."

"Does he know that he is going to be dumped?" Aponia asked unsure of how she felt about the situation.

"I don't think so. Far as I know, he told Ben yesterday that they might get married when she graduates." Loki stopped to check his friend. Her stone rubbing had stopped. "How are you doing?"

"I'm not sure," she answered honestly. Aponia practiced her deep breathing as she rubbed the calming stone in the same rhythm with her thumb. Loki relaxed back against the lattice wall watching as his friend regained control of her emotions. The therapist would be proud of the efforts Aponia was taking to control her anger.

Loki knew the steps well as he remembered what the therapist had memorialized in his memory. First, validate the experience. Loki knew how hard it had been for Aponia to share her truth with him and he had been honored to support her. It said to him that she trusted him and respected him. She was now giving herself time to accept and process information. Understanding the steps, Loki backed off and gave his friend whatever time she needed to absorb the information.

She also stroked the blue green stone with her thumb as if her life depended on it. And, from his perspective it did. This would help her to learn how to manage in the future. Loki had been down this road and knew it well. He was proud of himself for recognizing his friend's needs. His mother had been right, he was able to help. Aponia would have to continually monitor her symptoms when things happen if she wanted to operate normally in her life. Of course, the therapist would continue to help her cope. Loki continued to enjoy his sessions although that was not the case in the beginning.

A short time later, Rowdy waddled in making his presence known with his small raspy voice. Loki rubbed the pup and rolled him around on the floor like a small child. Aponia watched him curiously sure that Loki knew him.

"How are you doing, Rowdy boy?" Loki laughed as he picked the pup up and put him into his lap.

"How do you know him?" she asked reaching out to rub him as he sat contently in Loki's lap.

"He comes over after breakfast every morning to get scraps from my mother," he answered.

"What, he is a hustler," Aponia laughed chiding the pup for filching food from the neighbors. "We do feed our dog."

"Not a question. He just found out how to get an extra breakfast and some snuggles before returning home."

"Can't really blame him for that," she laughed uproariously. She could not remember feeling so care free in the recent past. It felt good to laugh and genuinely share her story with her old friend.

Loki stayed a while longer before returning to his home. He'd promised to protect her honor with their class mates when he could. Aponia felt honored that she had such a good and forgiving friend especially given her unfair treatment of him. Years ago, Loki had been over weight with acne, braces and self-esteem issues. Now, he was a broad shouldered young man who accepted who and what he was. Aponia admitted privately that he was also handsome with his smooth cinnamon skin, rich chocolate-colored eyes and straight white teeth. She knew that there would be some lucky girl in his future, if not already.

Chapter Nine

Over the next several weeks, Aponia and the therapist focused on dissecting the rage or anger into three stages. Stage one: onset or when Aponia could first identify that something was going on in her body. Stage two: temperature rising or when Aponia began to feel that emotions and behaviors were becoming out of control. And stage three: recovery or when Aponia began to regain control and manage her emotions. It was not an easy task. Aponia learned more about herself and began a journey of introspection that left her exhausted.

Aponia had not anticipated that looking inside would be so tiring. She did not understand why this was happening, but sought to understand how it was impacting her body. The therapist allowed her to cry when needed and celebrate when she had a break through. Aponia was beginning a new life. With the understanding came the outside exploration.

Aponia continued to interview her family and found new interest when her family traveled to the family's cemetery to clean the head stones on Memorial Day. This had been a chore that Aponia and her siblings detested. The people there were dead and gone in the cemetery. Why should they care what their graves looked like? Her contact with Mr. Billy intrigued and raised an awareness of the past and her ancestors that lived before her. Maybe it didn't matter to the dead, but it did to the living that honored them she thought to herself.

In the Honey Springs Cemetery, Uncle Rory with his strong booming voice and jovial personality served as the family keeper of family history and its secrets. Uncle Rory was considered a handsome man with smooth cocoa colored skin, dark wavy hair, pork chop side burns and a thick mustache. His wife, Stella, was a round woman with dark skin, white teeth and a bigger than life personality. They rarely were together at the cemetery, but at home Rory and Stella were known for their bawdy jokes and foul language. All said with love.

The Honey Springs Cemetery was laid out in groups of families. The African Americans were segregated to the rear of the cemetery. From what Aponia gathered from Uncle Rory, African American families were relegated to the back of the cemetery by more affluent members of the community who preferred being seen at the front of the cemetery. This was a fact that members of the community had accepted as the status quo. No one challenged this anymore, but the burial practice was clearly unfair to segments of the community who were seen as having no voice in the matter.

Uncle Rory used a cane in the cemetery occasionally leaning on the carved head of a wolf to take the weight off his injured knee. As a high school student, he had played football and paid the price into adulthood with a crooked knee. Aponia showed more interest than in years past. She was especially interested when he showed them the headstones for the Markham and Monarch families. Most headstones were situated with their family units including husbands, wives, their children, and children's wives.

The name Daniel Monarch and his wife, Kittie, caught her attention. The graves lay flat to the ground and were partially covered by grass and other vegetation. An old broken-down cattle fence was not far from the headstones. There was speculation that these graves had been relocated from family home sites that were taken by the government for Fort Gibson Lake.

Aponia knelt down and pulled grass and debris from the concrete rectangular stones. The one on the left read, William "Billy" Green, born 1825 and died 1901, 76 years. To his right, the second read "Hattie Green, born 1826 and died 1896, 70 years. Adults gathered around as Aponia lovingly stroked the headstones. Light breezes blew ruffling the sides of Aponia's curls. Closing her eyes, she knew that this was the right Mr. Billy. She couldn't prove the direct ties yet, but she knew it was him. Something whispered "well done" to her heart.

Her mother took photos of the headstones and they looked around for other family members in the immediate area. Headstones appeared to be positioned at regular intervals, but there were gaps where no stones appeared. Uncle Rory suspected that the stones may have been covered over with time by the tractor cutting down the grass. He found a metal post in a pile just beyond the fencing. Positioning the one and half inch metal post vertical to areas where graves were suspected to be underground, he began beating the post into the ground with a discarded piece of wood. Within seconds, the metal hit a rock or something hard underneath the earth. This happened four more times.

Uncle Rory enlisted the help of his nephew, a strong lanky young man of twenty years of age. Calvin took the proffered shovel and began digging. He quickly unearthed four rectangular headstones similar to the first two. Aponia took a small hand-held hoe and went to work removing years of dirt, grass and debris from their faces. One read "Alex Green, born 1935 and died 1961". The next read, "Dorian Green, born 1942 and died 1972." The remaining two read, "Daniel Monarch" and "Kittie Monarch". Something was familiar about the names, but Aponia could not be certain. This felt good and she was sure that this was her family.

Uncle Rory didn't have much information about William and Hattie Green other than she and her family were from Arkansas originally. According to what he'd been told as a child, they had been escaped slavery during the chaos of the Civil War and relocated in Indian Territory. Uncle Rory believed that there were several graves that had to be relocated from family land because the government acquired the farms for construction of Fort Gibson Lake.

A bright light and feeling of warmth passed through Aponia starting at her feet and moving up and out the top of her head. She didn't know what or why it was happening. She could not recall all the names given to her by Mr. Billy, but something was familiar. She kept saying the names over and over in her mind and recorded information and took photos of the headstones relating to her relatives.

When she and her therapist met, Aponia passed along information and photos that were taken from Honey Springs Cemetery. The therapist spread the family tree sheets out on the table of her office and reviewed each one by one. The photos of the headstones were matched up with the names on the family tree.

Daniel Monarch had married Kittie Green according to Mr. Billy and was confirmed by the headstones found in the cemetery. Kittie Green Monarch's obituary also confirmed these facts. Moreover, William and Hattie Green's headstones were found. This bolstered her therapist's theory that this was a viable connection to Aponia's family. In addition, there was a Dorian and Alex Green that matched with information provided by Mr. Billy. The therapist slowly took off her glasses, smiled widely and clapped her hands in celebration.

"That's it!" Aponia shouted pumping her fists in the air and hopping up and down alternating from one foot to the other.

The therapist enjoyed watching Aponia so happy, but wanted to slow her down and remind her of what it means to be a good investigator. "Whoah!" she held her hands in front of Aponia to slow her celebration. "We have to do our due diligence."

"What is due diligence?" Aponia asked. "And why do I have to do it?"

"Due diligence is taking steps to satisfy ourselves that these people indeed are the same people that we believe them to be," she explained. Aponia looked like she'd lost her best friend. "This is part of being good detectives. We have to find additional information from different sources to prove that they are who we think they are."

"What if there is nothing else to prove who they are?" she flopped in the scoop chair with her arms folded across her chest.

"We just do our best. Sometimes, we just try to eliminate facts by proving that they aren't others with the same name, date of birth or death. For example: What year were they born? Were they living in area where the family was reportedly living? Can we verify children or grandchildren?"

Aponia grumbled, "Sounds like a lot of more work." She spun the scoop chair around with her legs anchoring the movement. The therapist smiled and confirmed with a head nod that she agreed. Aponia didn't believe that they would ever have enough at the rate they were going.

Later that evening, Officer Bert Gleeson dropped by the Monarch home. Watching as he entered the small living room wearing his blue uniform and sun glasses pushed upon the top of his head, Valerie ushered him onto the sofa. Ethan, who just arrived to take Solomon to basketball practice, came into the living room and sat next to Valerie. Ethan was wearing board shorts and a white loose-fitting t-shirt as he sat. Valerie looked curious about what they might learn.

"We'd like to include Poni in whatever you've found," Valerie stated as Aponia wandered into the room and sat on a chair adjacent to the officer. The officer nodded his head in acknowledgment and started rifling through his papers. All watched and waited. Ethan asked that Solomon take Sophia out to play until all the information had been exchanged. Reluctantly, he left the room with a curious Sophia in tow. She craned her neck around trying to grasp bits of conversation as they left the room.

"Well, we talked with Jett Franklin, his mother and Mr. Dexter Palmer," Officer Gleeson began. All were quiet as he summarized their interviews. Jett Franklin maintained his story that he was never with your daughter. We were unable to dispute his story completely, although it was likely that he left with your daughter. Aponia stated that she overheard a conversation between Jett and a person he called Jay. The police obtained telephone records and called a classmate named Jenny Carpenter and verified her conversation with Jett Franklin. The call was inconclusive.

Aponia stopped the officer saying, "My name is Aponia, please refer to me by my name. I feel like a thing and not a person when you keep saying "your daughter".

Apologizing, Officer Gleeson continued with the results of his investigation. Jenny Carpenter confirmed that she had a conversation with Jett Franklin and that he was taking care of a problem. There was no mention of Aponia or him running away. According to his mother, Tesha Franklin stated that she was at work and unaware of any plan to run away by her son.

In short, the investigation is inconclusive where Jett Franklin is concerned. As for Dexter Palmer at the Gentry building, he called in an anonymous call to the police department regarding hearing a woman screaming and a dog barking in an apartment. He denies meeting Aponia or Jett that night. However, he confirmed that he had dealt with Jett in the past.

"How would Poni know about his apartment or what he looks like?" Ethan complained.

"Mr. Palmer reported that he is well known in the community especially with less than reputable tenants in the building," Officer Gleeson explained. "He says Jett has periodically rented rooms for a night or two in the building, so some of his classmates may be aware of his appearance and location in the building."

Since there were no keys in the room where Aponia was found, Officer Gleeson was unable to say conclusively that Mr. Dexter Palmer provided the room to Aponia. At the very least, Mr. Palmer saved Aponia's life by alerting authorities for medical assistance and the police department to a problem in his building. Ethan did not believe Jett or Mr. Dex for a moment; however, Mr. Dex did call for help. Aponia watched quietly rubbing her calming stone.

She finally asked, "Do you believe me Officer Gleeson?" Aponia looked directly into the brown eyes of the officer trying so desperately to maintain his detachment from the family.

He thought for a moment struggling with being honest or maintaining his objectivity with the family. Looking back at the assessing eyes of Aponia, he answered honestly, "I do believe what you reported and I know you believe it as well. My gut says that it happened just as you said. However, I am unable to go into court and say beyond a reasonable doubt that Jett caused the injuries that you sustained. Mr. Dex did nothing that we could find that was illegal."

Ethan brought his big fist down on the table murmuring a few unsavory words under his breath. Valerie cuddled Aponia into her arms and held her to her chest. Officer Gleeson felt for the family's position and wanted to tell them what they wanted to hear, but couldn't.

"Thank you for your honesty, Officer Gleeson," Aponia dislodged herself from her mother's arms. She knew he had tried his best and she understood things from his perspective. She didn't like the outcome, but there wasn't anything else to be done.

"I wish I could have been able to tell you that we would be arresting Jett Franklin for harming you, but I can't lie to you," he explained.

Aponia wondered how many times the officer had to deliver bad news to victims when he wished it could be otherwise. Just because she couldn't prove it, did not make it not happen. The truth was the truth and she did her best and that had to be enough. For that one fact, she was proud of herself. She also accepted her own responsibility in this situation because she was unable to deal with the anger that plagued her life. The silver lining of this situation was that her parents forced her to pursue mental health treatment.

Officer Gleeson waved goodbye to the family as he left and drove away in the black and white police car with the words Honey Springs Police written in block letters across the side. Valerie and Ethan both held their daughter for a time hoping that she used the tools that the therapist had provided her to get through these difficult times. Ethan later took Solomon to basketball practice at the school and invited Sophia to be an honorary assistant coach to give Aponia quiet time with her mother.

When all was quiet, Valerie pulled Aponia back onto the sofa to talk. Aponia didn't really want to talk but she listened to the words of encouragement and pride shared by her mother. Genuinely concerned, Valerie told Aponia that she sincerely believed what she had told them. She knew Jett had been culpable in her injuries, but did not focus on that fact.

"Thank you so much for believing me," Aponia cried. "I want to hate Jett and Mr. Dexter." She was reminded of Officer Gleeson's words that Mr. Dex called for medical assistance and the police that saved her life. That had to be enough as well.

"I will be forever thankful to Mr. Dex, but I know that he has a crime riddled reputation on Gentry Street," Valerie shared her thoughts. Aponia nodded and wanted to go out to the gazebo for quiet time.

Valerie watched Aponia walk out the back door allowing the screen door to slam behind her. Feeling helpless, Valerie called her best friend and Loki's mother. She filled her friend in on the results of the police investigation and asked for advice. Suggesting that Loki check on Aponia, his mother passed along the message to her son.

Aponia quietly seated herself in the gazebo furthest away from the rounded doorway into the gazebo and began to cry quietly into her hands. Rowdy whimpered at her feet trying hard to get her attention and to worm his way into her lap. Muffling her cries, she buried her face in her hands as she bent at her waist to hide her face.

A short time later, Loki arrived to find his friend in tears. He knew the reason for the tears because his mother had filled him in Not sure how to proceed, Loki sat down next to Aponia and listened quietly for a while.

Gaining confidence, he said softly, "I'm here if you want to talk." Aponia was embarrassed, but could not change course quick enough. "I know this is not easy, but I want to be here for you." He wrapped his arms around his friend and pulled her close to his chest. Tears broke his heart, but he held her as she squirmed against him. After a time, she relaxed and leaned into him crying in earnest.

This had been harder than Aponia had anticipated. She hated Jett, but this was not all his fault. He would have allowed men like Mr. Dex to touch her and probably more intimate things as well. She cried for what might have been. Then, she turned her attention to the cowardly choice to leave her in a pool of blood without a thought to her health or safety. He had assumed her dead. This was unconscionable. Now, she sat with a man that she had wronged so many years ago. It was all too confusing to Aponia. Finally, she sat up and away from Loki so that she could see his face.

"What did I do to deserve such a good friend?" Aponia smiled.

"Squirt, you always had me as a friend whenever you wanted," he smiled widely. "You never guessed why I would hang out with my best friend's little sister all those years."

"I don't understand," Aponia looked more intently into Loki's brown eyes. There was something there but she couldn't put her finger on it. He had been watching her of late from his bedroom window. Additionally, he had forgiven her for her transgression so many years earlier. Could he actually be feeling more for her that she had known?

"Think about it," he said sweetly. "You never considered how special you were to me? Never wondered why I defended you against our class mates?"

She was seeing Loki in a different light. Could he have tender feelings for her? Looking more closely, she asked a question that she was afraid he'd answer, "You have feelings for me? Like a woman and man feelings? Not just best friends?"

"You were always my best friend. But along the way, you became more to me." Loki was embarrassed to be telling her at this time, but wanted her to know his feelings. Aponia smiled and saw him for the first time. Maybe in the back of her mind, she may have wished for this herself. He kissed the tip of her nose. She folded herself into him feeling safe for the first time in a very long time. Jett had never really made her feel this way, safe, secure and loved for her own imperfect self. They enjoyed the moment. It was time to move forward with her new life.

Chapter Ten

In the weeks that followed, the therapist guided Aponia through news articles and other information that offered clues to her family's history. Ethan Monarch had not grown up with his grandparents, so he knew little of his mother's side of the family. He only remembered that his father and mother called her "Kat". A marriage certificate for Daniel Monarch confirmed that his wife's full name was Kittie Alexia Green. Her middle name had been a variation of her father's name, Alex.

Alex Green and his wife, Dorian, had been in Oklahoma since their youth. Alex's father was Fred Green and his grandfather, Arthur Green, relocated with his family from Arkansas as children. This aligned with the information provided by Mr. Billy.

As the pair worked at her round table, the therapist smiled widely at her apprentice. "I think we have enough information to unequivocally confirm that Kittie Alexia Green Monarch is indeed the same person as Mr. Billy's relative. They had finally proved beyond a reasonable doubt that Mr. William Green known as Mr. Billy was Aponia's fifth great grandfather found in the Honey Springs Cemetery.

"Whoo-hoo!" Aponia screamed pumping her arms up and down in celebration. "Finally, we know how we connect!" After more hip wagging and feet stomping, she started to slow as if a new question occurred to her. "Why did he contact me?"

The therapist explained that she wasn't absolutely sure, but had some theories based on the information that she found. "First, some of the newspapers mention a Green family cemetery not far from Honey

Springs. The information provided by your Uncle Rory indicates that the graves were relocated when Fort Gibson Lake was constructed. They align."

"If you are part of Mr. Billy's family and I believe you are. He said that he would not rest in peace until what was taken from his family was restored." Aponia put her head on her hands in deep thought. "The rage or anger problem started with him. He didn't know how to manage it until late in life and lost his family. Unfortunately, in life he was too late. Since then, he has tried to help his family, but for generations he was been unsuccessful. He never gave up because we know he reached out to you."

The wheels began to turn in Aponia's head, "So, if I am able to deal with that problem, I can change the course of my life. If I share his story and mine, then I can change the generations that follow me. If I can accomplish that, then he would have restored what was taken by the war. Mission accomplished and rest in peace." She waited expectantly for a confirmation from her therapist.

"Absolutely!" she yelled slapping palms high in the air with Aponia. This had been a journey of learning from within. Aponia was reminded of epigenetics and the importance of what had been passed down to she and her family. She read, "Epigenetics was the change in emotions, behaviors or different parts of the world without a change in DNA, the things that make up who we are."

"So, you're saying that it's possible to pass things down from one generation to another without changing the strands that make up who we are," Aponia struggled to understand. "Mr. Billy passed down this rage because of slavery and the Battle of Honey Springs that he had experienced. He didn't mean to pass it down, but it happened."

"That's what I believe," the therapist put her arm around Aponia's slim shoulders. "Mr. Billy didn't know how to help himself until later in life and he has been trying to change things for the generations that follow. His sons and daughters dealt with it by hiding behind alcohol, drugs, and some had mental health breaks." She wanted to cry for those that Mr. Billy were not able to help.

"So, how or why was I different?" Aponia asked genuinely trying to understand. Mr. Billy had tried to help generations that preceded her without success. She knew something was different, but needed to ensure that what she learned about the rage and anger was passed on.

"Your family recognized that they could no longer run from a problem that they were seeing. Your parents brought you to me for therapy where we could pull things apart that were hiding inside you. This helped you to not only understand yourself, but empathize with the ancestors that came before you. This will help you to successfully pass on what you've learned to others."

"I don't truly feel like I understand how all the parts fit together."

The therapist squeezed her tightly, "You understand more than you know." Aponia left her office feeling like weights had been lifted from her shoulders. She also felt that there were things that needed to be done before she felt she could truly feel that she accomplished what Mr. Billy needed to rest in peace.

When Aponia went out to the gazebo, she had so many pleasant thoughts to hold in her heart. First, Loki had shared his true feelings about her and she was over the moon for him. He had been able to empathize with her feelings because he too had been in therapy. Accepting that she was special just as she was made Aponia's confidence soar. She didn't need to try to be perfect to be accepted, he liked her just as she was. Life had changed in such a short time.

She turned her attention to Mr. Billy. Thinking out loud, she asked what she needed to do to fulfill what he needed to rest in peace. Stroking the stone, she closed her eyes and breathed deeply trying to connect with Mr. Billy. The breeze fluttered the blossoms of the honey suckle plants causing the smell to intensify around her. Listening, she wanted to hear what was around her. A soft voice spoke to her heart saying, "You are special because you are mine."

Aponia smiled and listened more. "This unchecked rage cost me generations of my children and grandchildren. It stops with you because you listened and responded."

"I didn't really," Aponia explained quietly. "I was forced into treatment by my parents. You know I challenged the therapist at every turn. I feel like that I caused a lot of problems that didn't need to happen."

The voice answered back to her heart, "You did what needed to be done to get help for yourself. You are exactly who you are and that means your path is not always straight. You have to prove to yourself that it is right for you."

Continuing to argue the wisdom of challenging every decision at every turn, she finally grasped what he had been saying. Aponia had never been one to quietly accept authority or decisions that she did not understand. Mr. Billy understood and anticipated that this would be her path. Because she challenged decisions and was willing to learn from her mistakes, she would pass her knowledge to the next generation and accept that they may also not accept the status quo.

Whispering into her heart, a soft voice said, "I am proud of you and you will make those that come after you proud as well. Be well." Afterward, all was quiet and Aponia sat quietly rubbing her stone. Rowdy came in barking wildly and twitching his little tail. She scooped him up into her arms and began dancing around in circles. Because of this ordeal, she had found Rowdy. He had become a vital part of their family.

To capture her experiences with Jett and her journey dealing with the rage, she began writing in a journal. Beginning with her own personal experiences, she captured the events and outbursts that plagued her childhood to the present.

Vowing to be true to herself, she documented her decision to run away with Jett and the circumstances leading to her injuries. Including her interpretation of her encounters with Mr. Billy, she presented what was lost and what would lead to him resting in peace. The most intricate portion included the genealogy of her family and the due diligence required to investigate and authenticate their results. This was her legacy to the next generation and she wanted them to understand why the journey was so important.

Aponia assumed that those that came after her would also enjoy challenges and require authentication of her results. It was too important for things to be forgotten by Aponia or her family as they grew and went on with their lives. This was just too important to not collect and preserve. She would not feed the rage allowing it to die a slow death using the strategies and tools learned in therapy.

Chapter Eleven

The following weekend, Aponia walked to the end of block to the Honey Springs Community Center, a tan colored brick building surrounded by jungle gym equipment, a tennis court, a basketball court, and a soccer field, where many young people hung out. As she neared the basketball court, young men in varying states of fitness ran from one end of the concrete basketball court to the other. Ten-foot basketball goals with red, white and blue nets were affixed to each on either end of the court. Aponia recognized Jett's long lanky body standing on the sidelines heckling other players. As she neared, his head turned and his eyes bugged out as if he'd seen a ghost.

Aponia refused to shrink back and run away. Because Honey Springs was a small town, she knew the day would come when she would run into Jett. Today was that day and she would not slink away like she'd done something wrong. Others stopped to watch the interaction. Others continued to play their games without much interest in the drama playing out on the sidelines.

"What are you doing here?" he stuttered. "I was told not to talk to you by my mother's lawyer friend." He stuck his hands in his pockets and pretended not to see her. She had questions and wanted answers.

"I came here to ask you two questions," Aponia stated unmoved by his attempt to dismiss her. Jett didn't answer, but she could tell by the clenching of his jaw muscles he was feeling some sort of guilt. "I understand that the police have dismissed my case so you have no legal worries from me."

"I wasn't there," he finally said waving over to his friend.

"We both know that you were," Aponia smiled watching his expression turn to sadness.

"What do you want from me?" he asked resigned. "I said I wasn't there. There are no answers for you here."

"Answers to two questions," she stated unmoved. "First, why did you leave me?"

His head turned toward Aponia and he looked like a much younger child, "I didn't know what to do. I got scared and ran because I thought you were dead. I knew my mom thought I was at home so it was safe to say I had been there all night."

"Did it ever occur to you to just say no when I asked you to run away with me?"

"No, I brought it up months before about running away. And, well I'm a guy and I didn't want you to think I was weak or something." Aponia thought about what he'd said and looked at his impossibly young face and knew he'd been telling her the truth. "So, what now?"

"Did you really intend to let other men touch me intimately?" she asked curiously. This question had been nagging her for weeks.

"I'm a guy," he began. "I knew you were attracted to me and that I could get away with anything. So, I knew that you could get a free place to stay if you allowed some intimacies. I didn't intend to stay with you so I really wasn't concerned what they did to you." This answer hurt more than any that Aponia had imagined in her mind. There was the truth. He just didn't care what happened to her. Unfortunately, she and her future could have been sacrificed without much thought. She wanted to make snide comments, but couldn't. She had asked the questions and he had answered. Inside her pocket, she rubbed the calming stone maintaining her control.

"What now?" he asked tiring of the conversation.

"Nothing," Aponia turned to leave. "You answered my questions and we're done. I learned that getting angry at you would only be a distraction for what was inside me. I just had to ask you those questions for myself before I could let it go. We are done."

Jett, who'd sworn that he'd never talk to her, stated quietly, "I'm sorry."

"Thank you," she answered back genuinely as she left the basketball court headed home. The therapist had been right. Jett hadn't done the right thing, but he'd reacted like a kid who got scared and went home to hide. Aponia now understood that he had not tried to hurt her nor did he care what happened to her at others' hands. He did try to take advantage of her situation and allow men to touch her. After she was hurt, he reacted like a scared kid. That is just what he was, a scared kid."

The people in the crowd returned their attention to the game. The crowd parted for Aponia to leave. Within the group, Loki came up behind Aponia and threw his arm casually around her shoulder. Some of his class mates made kissing noises as they walked away. He walked her to the corner.

He laughed and said happily, "I'm proud of you. He didn't know what hit him. And when Jenny gets through with him, he'll feel even lower than a coyote trying to crawl under an ant." The visual made her smile.

"Thanks," she answered. "It hurt, but I think I'm done with it." The two made jokes and walked home together.

That evening as Aponia meditated and stroked her calming stone in the gazebo, she began to feel more in control of her life. Loki told her that Jenny had dumped Jett in front of the entire basketball team. Jett actually cried and ran home. It was petty of her, but she laughed until she cried. In a short time, people stopped asking if she was feeling better and she began feeling more like her old self.

Aponia had asked her father to purchase a tree that she could plant in the backyard. Ethan allowed her to select the tree, a small Japanese Maple with reddish gold foliage. This was to be her memory tree to symbolize her growth past this point in her life. Ethan dug the hole for daughter and left the planting for Aponia.

Aponia prepared three pieces of paper with the following words: "outbursts", "rage/anger", and "trauma" written on each. Wrapping each piece of paper around a small stone, she buried each stone in the hole with the tree. Vowing to let the past be the past, Aponia prayed a short prayer, buried them and released them from her life journey. She covered the roots of the tree with the dirt her father had removed from the hole.

Tamping the damp soil around the base of the tree, Aponia smiled at her memory tree. It was time for the celebration. Aponia removed her shoes and socks. Dancing to her own internal soundtrack, Aponia began waving her arms round and round, jumping up and down in celebration. Joining the celebration, Sophia kicked off her shoes and joined the dancing. This was their earth dance, allowing the negative energy to pass into the earth to be converted to positive energy by the earth. Loki secretly watched the celebration from his second-floor bedroom. He liked to see Aponia happier than he could remember.

On their next Memorial Day, Aponia and her family went to the Honey Springs Cemetery to clean the graves and honor those that had come before. She and other teenagers joined with the adults clearing and decorating graves with flowers. Ordinarily, she would not have paid attention to Uncle Rory's history lessons, but today was different. The hairs on her arm stood up and something had come alive inside her. She couldn't explain what she was feeling but it was making her skin tingle. This was her time to honor those that came before and share Mr. Billy's story. Additionally, she would share her story as well.

When she and her cousins came to the graves of William and Hattie Green, Aponia shared the story of Mr. Billy and how she'd come to know him in the hospital. She didn't think any would be interested in what she'd experienced, but they were. One cousin actually wanted to read the journal entries and learn about their family, slavery and the soldier that went from enslaved to war hero in the Battle of Honey Springs. He served his country and what he believed in so that his children could escape the manacles of slavery. This was his legacy standing before him. Aponia felt compelled to share his story and then share her own. This was her family and she was proud.

A breeze ruffled Aponia's hair and a voice deep in her heart whispered, "I am with you. Don't be afraid." Aponia cleared her throat as all eyes continued on her. It was not like her to seek the focus of attention. This was bigger than her or any one person. Their family deserved to know what great things her family had accomplished. Revealing the incredible journey of Mr. Billy during his flight from slavery and his victory on the battlefield was exciting and inspiring. She could feel Mr. Billy's spirit smiling. "After the war, Mr. Billy was left with anger and rage that he had no idea how to control. This rage destroyed his family and has for many generations." Eyes were locked on her every word. She was sure that they believed her and were sympathetic to what she was saying but she needed to hear it.

Uncle Rory leaned forward on his cane and listened as Aponia shared her story and that of Mr. Billy. He too could not have been prouder of Mr. Billy's legacy. They would now maintain the very back of the cemetery unearthing all the headstones that had been over grown and forgotten. Uncle Rory too would be sharing their stories as the family historian. He had learned from Aponia and Mr. Billy vowing to keep those memories alive.

Uncle Rory's big hand came to rest on her shoulder. "There is no doubt it happened. Most people don't have the courage to stand up and share what happened to them. I'm proud of you." Aponia buried her face in Uncle Rory's shoulder. It was such a relief to share that with people who didn't question her sanity.

Aponia gathered herself and said as a comment to herself as well as those listening, "Because of him and his story, I was forced to get help. Those that came before did not always have an option to get help. I am glad I did although I was forced in the beginning." Aponia smiled back thinking of how she had fought therapy and behaved abhorrently to the therapist. Yes, she had truly been forgiven.

Aponia and Uncle Rory gathered flowers and placed them on the graves around the headstones. In her heart, she answered, "Your welcome." Mr. Billy would become Grandpa Billy resting happily in peace. Aponia vowed to come back each year to share her updated story with him. Because of him, she understood more about what made her uniquely Aponia Arminda Monarch, protector of their family history.

Aponia kneeled next to his headstone, kissed the tips of her right hand and placed it delicately on the edge as if touching Grandpa Billy's cheek. Spreading a bouquet of flowers on the graves of her fifth great grandfather William Green and his wife Hattie Green, Aponia proclaimed that Grandpa Billy could now rest in peace knowing that the next generation was equipped to restore what had been taken away so many years before. "We got you!"

Additional Information and Resources

Dear Readers:

If you enjoyed **Rage that Spans Generations** and would like additional information regarding the resources used, please find a list below:

For the Battle of Honey Springs:

Oklahoma Historical Society   https://www.okhistory.org/
                                     sites/honeysprings

Battle of Honey Springs Report   https://okhistory.org/
                                     sites/forms/hsreport.pdf

Honey Springs Battlefield and Museum

423159 E. 1030 Road

Checotah, OK 74426

honeysprings@history.ok.gov

Fort Gibson National Cemetery

https://www.cem.va.gov/cems/nchp/ftgibson.asp

Trail of Tears

Paul's, Elizabeth Prine. "Trail of Tears". Encyclopedia Britannica, 6 Oct. 2022, https://www.britannica.com/event/Trail-of-Tears.

Accessed 18 February 2023.

Emancipation

Pruitt-Yung, Sharon. "Slavery Didn't End on Juneteenth. What

You Should Know About This important Day." https://www.npr.org/2021/06/17/1007315228/juneteenth-   w h a t - is-origin-observation

Resources for dealing with trauma:

At least one in seven children have experienced child abuse and/or neglect in the past year. Trauma is a serious mental health concern that should be recognized and addressed. This book does not attempt to minimize or rationalize the devastating symptoms of trauma, its impact or treatment.

For information and resources related to childhood trauma, please refer to the Substance Abuse and Mental Health Services Administration (SAMHSA) website at https://www.samhsa.gov/child-trauma/understanding-child-trauma.

It is the author's hope that readers are prompted to seek professional help to assist with recognizing the signs of trauma or obtaining assistance.

www.ingramcontent.com/pod-product-compliance
Lightning Source LLC
Chambersburg PA
CBHW051533120626
46551CB00012B/1206